German Grammar in a

Deutsche Grammatik –
kurz und schmerzlos

Langenscheidt

German Grammar in a Nutshell

Deutsche Grammatik – kurz und schmerzlos

Von Christine Stief
und Christian Stang

Langenscheidt

Berlin · München · Wien · Zürich · New York

Erläuterung der Sonderzeichen/Explanation of the symbols:

 = *Tip* / Tipp

 = *Help* / Hilfe

 = *Attention* / Achtung

Abkürzungen/Abbreviations:

ff.	= *and the following [pages]* /	folgende Seiten
f.	= *and the following [page]* /	folgende Seite
p.	= *page* /	Seite
sb.	= *somebody* /	jemand(en)
sth.	= *something* /	etwas

Umwelthinweis: gedruckt auf chlorfrei gebleichtem Papier

Umschlaggestaltung: Independent Medien-Design
Zeichnungen im Innenteil: Marlene Pohle, Stuttgart
Englische Übersetzungen: Editorial Services Williams
Lektorat: Marion Techmer, Christian Frieser

© 2002 by Langenscheidt KG, Berlin und München
Druck: Druckhaus Langenscheidt, Berlin
Printed in Germany
ISBN 3-468-34949-1
www.langenscheidt.de

02
03
04
05
06
5.
4.
3.
2.
1.

Inhalt
Contents

Inhalt

Inhalt

Vorwort
Introduction

Maybe you've considered German grammar to be difficult – up to now. This short and entertaining little book will show you that this is not quite so and that German grammar can be quite fun! It has been specially designed to help non-native speakers of German to master the basic rules of the language. As briefly and painlessly as possible. It makes no pretence at being *exhaustive*, since that might also prove to be *exhausting* and counterproductive as a result.

The book is based on the *Zertifikat Deutsch*, the main two aims of which are to promote the communicative use of language and to provide a recognised standard for adult learners of German. The grammar content is based on general everyday usage in the German-speaking countries of Germany, Austria and Switzerland. All the headings, explanations, tips and reminders have been written in English. To make things even easier we have also translated the German examples illustrating the rules into English, too. The numbering system makes it easy to find your way and to repeat or revise material in any order.

An important new feature in this grammar book is its communicative approach. It's not the bare rules of grammar that take prominence but the way elements of language function as a means of communication. "What is my partner saying to me and how is he/she saying it?"

German Grammar in a Nutshell is practical, easy to understand and amusing, so you should have no great difficulty in "cracking" it! The motto being: the more unusual the situation, the better you remember the rule.

And one last tip: Don't try to devour the whole book at once! Despite its light and airy presentation it might prove to be too much to digest and spoil your appetite. Much better to enjoy the menu in small manageable portions and still have room for more!

The authors and publishers wish you every success with the book and hope you enjoy using it.

1 Der Artikel
The Article

oder

Gegenstände und Personen bestimmen
How to define things and people

*Peter: Hello, Alan. Welcome to Germany. I'm so glad you've come.
Are those your things? – Alan: Yes, the suitcase, the rucksack and the bag
are mine. – Peter: And the bike? – Alan: No, the bike doesn't belong
to me.*

In German, as in English, nouns (**Substantive***) are not normally used on their own. They are almost always preceded by an article (**Artikel**):

der Koffer, **der** Computer	*the suitcase, the computer*
das Fahrrad, **das** Handy	*the bike, the mobile phone*
die Tasche, **die** Zeitung	*the bag, the newspaper*

In German the definite article (**bestimmter Artikel**) tells us three things about the noun depending on how it is used in the sentence:

■ the gender: either **masculine** (**der**), **neuter** (**das**) or **feminine** (**die**)

■ the number: **singular** or **plural**

and also something typical for the German language:

■ the case: **nominative** (nom.), **accusative** (acc.), **dative** (dat.) or **genitive** (gen.)

Das ist **der** Koffer. (masculine, singular, nom.)	*That's the suitcase.*
Ich trage **den** Koffer. (masculine, singular, acc.)	*I'll carry the suitcase.*
Er kommt mit **dem** Zug. (masculine, singular, dat.)	*He's coming by train.*

In German, as in English, there are different kinds of article, as you'll see on the following pages.

---

* List of Grammatical Terms see Appendix, p. 174 ff.

1.1 Der unbestimmte und der bestimmte Artikel
The Indefinite and the Definite Article
<u>oder</u> *Ein Mann – der Mann, eine Frau – die Frau*

Hast du vielleicht einen Regenschirm?

Ja, der Regenschirm ist im Seitenfach des Rucksacks. Hier.

Super, ich habe meinen nämlich im Auto liegen lassen.

Peter: Have you got an umbrella? – Alan: Yes, the umbrella is in the side-pocket of the rucksack. Here. – Peter: Great. I've left mine in the car.

When do we use the indefinite and definite articles?

- The indefinite article (**ein, eine**) is used just like the English *a/an* if there is only one object or person or if something is new, unknown or non-specific.

- The definite article (**der, die, das**) normally refers just like the English *the* to something particular or something we already know.

> Es war einmal **ein** König. Der König hatte **eine** Tochter.
> **Die** Tochter hatte **ein** Pferd ...
> Im Büro: „Ich brauche **einen** Taschenrechner." – „Nimm doch **den**
> Rechner im Computer."
>
> *Once upon a time there was a king. The king had a daughter.*
> *The daughter had a horse.*
> *In the office: "I need a pocket calculator." – "Use the calculator in the*
> *computer."*

The negative form of the indefinite article **ein, eine** is **kein, keine:**

> Hast du **einen** Regenschirm?   *Have you got an umbrella?*
> Nein, ich habe **keinen**   *No, I haven't got an umbrella.*
> Regenschirm.

The negative of the definite article is formed with **nicht,** which is placed
before the article:

> Hier kommt **der** Bus.   *Here comes the bus.*
> Das ist **nicht der** Bus ins   *That's not the bus to the town*
> Stadtzentrum.   *centre.*

1.2   Formen des Artikels
Forms of the Article
oder Der Mann, den Mann ...

In German articles change their form depending on how the nouns they
belong to are used in the sentence. They indicate as we mentioned above
gender, number and case. The different forms look like this:

	singular			plural
	masculine	neuter	feminine	
nom.	der Mann	das Kind	die Frau	die Leute
	ein	ein	eine	(–)
	kein	kein	keine	keine
acc.	den	das	die	die
	einen	ein	eine	(–)
	keinen	kein	keine	keine
dat.	dem	dem	der	den
	einem	einem	einer	(–)
	keinem	keinem	keiner	keinen
gen.	des	des	der	der
	eines	eines	einer	(–)
	keines	keines	keiner	keiner

Don't worry. It really isn't as difficult as it may look. The good news is that all these endings are more or less the same for nouns, pronouns and adjectives. They can be reduced to a fairly simple table of key signals.

 Remember the following key signals:

	masculine	neuter	feminine	plural
nom.	*r*	*s*	*e*	*e*
acc.	*n*	*s*	*e*	*e*
dat.	*m*	*m*	*r*	*n*
gen.	*s*	*s*	*r*	*r*

 There is no indefinite article in the plural:

Diana braucht **einen** Regenschirm.	*Diana needs an umbrella.*
Tony verkauft Regenschirme.	*Tony sells umbrellas.*

Here are some more points to remember that will help you:

■ The plural form is always the same for all genders.

■ All the endings for nominative and accusative are the same, except for the masculine singular.

■ The endings for masculine und neuter are very often the same.

■ The endings for feminine und plural are always the same, except for the dative.

 In lots of expressions the article is combined with a preposition:

am *(an + dem)*	**Am** Freitag kommt der neue Kollege. *Our new colleague arrives on Friday.*
ans *(an + das)*	Frau Mathieu heftet den Zettel **ans** schwarze Brett. *Frau Mathieu pins the note to the notice-board.*
aufs *(auf + das)*	Wir warten **aufs** Frühstück. *We're waiting for breakfast.*
beim *(bei + dem)*	Herr Peters raucht oft **beim** Telefonieren. *Herr Peters often smokes while telephoning.*
im *(in + dem)*	Die Präsentation machen wir **im** Hotel „Vier Jahreszeiten". *We're doing the presentation in the "Four Seasons" Hotel.*
ins *(in + das)*	Heute gehen wir **ins** Kino. *Today we're going to the cinema.*
vom *(von + dem)*	Herr Runge kommt direkt **vom** Flughafen zu uns. *Herr Runge is coming here straight from the airport.*

zum *(zu + dem)*	Herr Miller fährt mit dem Taxi **zum** Flughafen. *Herr Miller is taking a taxi to the airport.*
zur *(zu + der)*	Frau Dupont fährt mit dem Fahrrad **zur** Arbeit. *Frau Dupont goes to work by bike.*

And just one more small piece of information to end with: the following words **dieser, jeder, jener, mancher, solcher, welcher** are all declined in the same way as the definite article **der**.

1.3 Der Nullartikel
The Zero Article
<u>oder</u> *Manchmal gehts auch ohne*

Sometimes, in certain expressions, the noun is used without any article at all:

Herr Giacobbe fährt gerne Zug.	*Herr Giacobbe likes travelling by train.*
Frau Mozahebi ist Ingenieurin.	*Frau Mozahebi is an engineer.*
Die neue Chefin hat nie Zeit.	*The new boss never has any time.*

There is no article, for example, used with:

Proper names

Frau Bodet und Herr Merkle fahren nach München.
Frau Bodet and Herr Merkle are travelling to Munich.
Das ist Tina, meine Schwester.
That's Tina, my sister.

Occupations

Frau Syrova ist Programmiererin.
Frau Syrova is a computer programmer.

Nationalities

Robin Preuß ist Schweizer, Amir Mozahebi ist Deutscher.
Robin Preuß is Swiss, Amir Mozahebi is German.

Cities, (most) countries, continents

Unser Web-Designer kommt aus Indien.
Our web-designer comes from India.

Abstract ideas (sometimes)

Die Professorinnen kämpfen für Gleichberechtigung.
The female professors are fighting for equality.

Materials (sometimes)

Herr Radwan trinkt in der Kantine nie Bier.
Herr Radwan never drinks beer in the cantine.

Set phrases/idiomatic expressions

Die Reporterin holt tief Atem.
The reporter takes a deep breath.

Headlines and titles

Ministertreffen verschoben
Ministers' meeting postponed

EXERCISE 1 * Please complete the following sentences with the correct form of the definite or indefinite article or no article at all.

1. Herr Blum hat _____ neue Assistentin. _____ Assistentin kommt aus _____ Berlin.

2. Herr Bodet ist _____ Marketingdirektor.

3. _____ alte Computerprogramm war langsamer.

4. Frau Radwan fährt heute mit ihrem Kollegen nach _____ Hamburg.

5. Herr Stix ist _____ Österreicher.

6. _____ Kopierer ist schon wieder kaputt.

7. _____ Tina macht einen Sprachkurs in _____ Spanien.

8. Während der Besprechung gab es nur _____ Kekse.

9. _____ Kolleginnen im Call-Center müssen _____ Geduld aufbringen.

10. Die Sekretärin buchte _____ Flug nach _____ Paris.

11. _____ Teamassistentin bestellt _____ Toner und _____ Papier.

12. Frau Kolar fand im Besprechungszimmer _____ Handy.

13. Herr Hundt hat _____ neuen Kollegen. _____ Kollege kommt aus Leipzig.

14. Frau Danz schreibt _____ Bericht. _____ Bericht muss morgen fertig sein.

15. Hat _____ Firma _____ Webseite? Nein, die Firma hat wirklich _____ Webseite.

* Key to the Exercises, see Appendix, p. 177 ff.

2 Das Substantiv
Nouns

oder

Gegenstände und Personen benennen
Giving names to objects and people

Alan: The car is new, isn't it? – Peter: Yes. The old one was spending too much time in the garage for repairs. – Alan: And you're happy with this one? – Peter: Yes, the fuel consumption is low, the engine is quiet and it's got a very big boot.

Nouns are used to give names to people, objects and things, as well as abstract ideas and are always written with a capital letter in German:

der **K**ollege, der **F**reund	*colleague, friend*
die **K**atze, die **R**ose	*cat, rose*
der **F**rieden, die **L**iebe	*peace, love*

2.1 Das Genus
Gender
<u>oder</u> *Aller guten Dinge sind drei*

In German every noun has a grammatical gender. The gender is shown by the article in front of the noun:

masculine	**der** Baum, **der** Kollege	*tree, colleague*
neuter	**das** Handy, **das** Mädchen	*mobile phone, girl*
feminine	**die** Blume, **die** Kollegin	*flower, colleague*

The grammatical gender of a noun and the biological gender are usually the same:

| **die** Frau, **die** Kollegin (feminine) | *woman, (female) colleague* |
| **der** Mann, **der** Kollege (masculine) | *man, (male) colleague* |

But there are exceptions:

| **das** Mädchen, **das** Kind (neuter) | *girl, child* |

Otherwise the choice of grammatical gender for a noun does not follow a logical set of rules. It is advisable, therefore, always to learn nouns together with the correct article. Luckily there are a few simple rules that apply to certain kinds of nouns that can help you remember.

■ Masculine are:

Male persons, male jobs/occupations, male animals

der Onkel, der Vater	*uncle, father*
der Ingenieur, der Grafiker	*(male) engineer, (male) designer*
der Löwe, der Hund	*lion, dog*

Days of the week, months, seasons

der Montag, der Dienstag	*Monday, Tuesday*
der Januar, der Februar	*January, February*
der Frühling, der Sommer	*Spring, summer*

Most nouns with the following endings

-and/-ant	der Doktor**and**, der Elef**ant**
	doctoral candidate, elephant
-ent	der Stud**ent**, der Pati**ent**
	student, patient
-er	der Comput**er**, der Besuch**er**
	computer, visitor
-ig	der Ess**ig**, der Hon**ig**
	vinegar, honey
-ismus	der Tour**ismus**, der Terror**ismus**
	tourism, terrorism
-ist	der Spezial**ist**, der Poliz**ist**
	specialist, policeman
-ling	der Früh**ling**, der Lehr**ling**
	spring, apprentice
-or	der Mot**or**, der Reakt**or**
	motor, reactor

■ Neuter are:

Many nouns with the prefix *Ge-* at the beginning

das **Ge**müse, das **Ge**birge   *vegetables, mountains*

The infinitive forms of verbs acting as nouns

das Essen, das Rauchen   *eating, smoking*

All nouns ending in

-chen	das Mäd**chen**, das Bröt**chen** *girl, bread roll*
-lein	das Büch**lein**, das Ring**lein** *little book, little ring*

A lot of nouns ending in

-nis	das Verzeich**nis**, das Geheim**nis** *register, secret*
-ment	das Medika**ment**, das Instru**ment** *medicine, instrument*
-o	das Bür**o**, das Aut**o** *office, car*
-t(r)um	das Wachs**tum**, das Stadtzen**trum** *growth, town centre*

■ Feminine are:

Female persons, female jobs/occupations and female animals

die Tante, die Kollegin   *aunt, (female) colleague*
die Anwältin, die Architektin   *(female) lawyer, (female) architect*
die Kuh, die Katze   *cow, cat*

Many flowers and trees

die Rose, die Tanne	*rose, fir tree*

Most nouns ending in

-ei	die Bücher**ei**, die Part**ei**	*library, party*
-enz	die Konfer**enz**, die Exist**enz**	*conference, existence*
-heit	die Frei**heit**, die Gesund**heit**	*freedom, health*
-keit	die Möglich**keit**, die Geschwindig**keit**	*possibility, speed*
-ie	die Industr**ie**, die Demokrat**ie**	*industry, democracy*
-ik	die Fabr**ik**, die Polit**ik**	*factory, politics*
-in	die Chef**in**, die Trainer**in**	*(female) boss, (female) trainer*
-ion	die Reg**ion**, die Nat**ion**	*region, nation*
-schaft	die Wirt**schaft**, die Wissen**schaft**	*economy, science*
-tät	die Quali**tät**, die Produktivi**tät**	*quality, productivity*
-ung	die Einlad**ung**, die Vertret**ung**	*invitation, stand-in*

E X E R C I S E   2   Please add the correct article to these nouns.

_____ Freundschaft, _____ Häuschen, _____ Zwilling, _____ Katalysator,

_____ Freiheit, _____ Erziehung, _____ Mechanismus, _____ Schülerin,

_____ Musik, _____ Brüderlein, _____ Verspätung, _____ Station,

_____ Präsident, _____ Biologie, _____ Kleinigkeit, _____ Fabrikant,

_____ König, _____ Radio, _____ Verwandtschaft, _____ Visum,

_____ Winter, _____ Chef, _____ Instrument, _____ Druckerei,

_____ Universität, _____ Mädchen, _____ Sortiment

2.2 Der Numerus
Singular and Plural
<u>oder</u> *Mehr als eins*

Peter: The tank is almost empty, I'll have to stop for petrol. It won't take long. And clean the windscreen as well. – Alan: Fine by me. I forgot to buy a newspaper at the station anyway, and I wanted a few peppermints, too.

Normally every noun has a singular and a plural form. The accompanying article has to indicate this. Fortunately, in the plural the definite article is always the same – it doesn't matter whether the noun in the singular is masculine, neuter of feminine, the article in the plural is always *die.* The indefinite article in the plural is even easier: there isn't one (see p. 16ff.).

The following table will help you to remember.

der/ein Mann	**die/** – Männer	*man, men*
das/ein Kind	**die/** – Kinder	*child, children*
die/eine Frau	**die/** – Frauen	*woman, women*

You have to remember, of course, that as a general rule nouns change their form in the plural. The following table shows you the different ways in which this can happen, with a few examples.

singular	plural	plural ending	applies to
1 a *der Löff**el*** *spoon* *das Zeich**en*** *sign* *das Mess**er*** *knife* *das Mäd**chen*** *girl* *das Büch**lein*** *little book*	*die Löffel* *spoons* *die Zeichen* *signs* *die Messer* *knives* *die Mädchen* *girls* *die Büchlein* *little books*	**–**	many nouns ending in **-el, -en, -er, -chen, -lein**
1 b *der Vater* *father* *die Mutter* *mother*	*die Väter* *fathers* *die Mütter* *mothers*	**–**, with **Umlaut**	many nouns ending in **-el, -en, -er, -chen, -lein**
2 a *der Schuh* *shoe*	*die Schuhe* *shoes*	**-e**	many nouns with only one syllable
2 b *der Sohn* *son* *der Baum* *tree*	*die Söhne* *sons* *die Bäume* *trees*	**-e** with **Umlaut**	many nouns with only one syllable

singular	plural	plural ending	applies to
3 die Tasche *bag* die Lehrerin *teacher*	die Taschen *bags* die Lehrerinnen *teachers*	**-n** **-nen**	feminine nouns ending in **-e, -in**
4 a das Bild *picture* das Kind *child*	die Bilder *pictures* die Kinder *children*	**-er**	many nouns with only one syllable
4 b das Haus *house* das Blatt *leaf*	die Häuser *houses* die Blätter *leaves*	**-er** with **Umlaut**	many nouns with only one syllable
5 das Auto *car* das Kino *cinema*	die Autos *cars* die Kinos *cinemas*	**-s**	many words from other languages

 Always learn a noun together with its article and the plural form. For example: **die Regel, Regeln** *(rule, rules)*.

EXERCISE 3   Please add the correct plurals.

1. die Reise   die _____

2. das Video   die _____

3. der Brief   die _____

4. die Kassette   die _____

5. das Brötchen   die _____   ▶

6. der Tag   die _____

7. der Bohrer   die _____

8. die Brille   die _____

9. das Motorrad   die _____

10. der Stift   die _____

11. der Trainee   die _____

12. das Jahr   die _____

13. die Sekretärin   die _____

14. das Zimmer   die _____

15. der Drucker   die _____

2.3 Der Kasus
Case Endings
oder Auf jeden Fall vier Fälle

Unlike English, German has retained case endings for nouns indicating the grammatical role they play in a sentence. Without them the meaning of the sentence would be unclear. In German nouns are used in four different "cases": **Nominativ** (nominative), **Akkusativ** (accusative), **Dativ** (dative) and **Genitiv** (genitive). Each case indicates what part a noun plays in a sentence: the subject, object etc. The case is determined by the verb or by prepositions.

Case	Role being played in the sentence	What to ask
nom.	subject; subject's complement **Herr Bräuer** ist mein Vorgesetzter. *Herr Bräuer is my superior.*	**Wer?, Was?** *Who? What?*
acc.	"standard" object (similar to direct object in some languages but not identical) Frau Schmitt liest **einen Bericht**. *Frau Schmitt is reading a report.*	**Wen?, Was?** *Who(m)? What?*
	after some prepositions Das Protokoll ist für **den Chef**. *The minutes are for the boss.*	
dat.	"special" object (similar to indirect object in some languages but not identical) Die Pizza schmeckt **mir**. *I like this pizza.*	**Wem?** *To whom?*
	after some prepositions Er nimmt sein Handy aus **der Tasche**. *He takes his mobile phone out of the bag.*	
gen.	shows mostly a possessive relationship, and is rarely used after some (mostly old-fashioned) prepositions Das Büro **meines Vaters**. *My father's office.* Aufgrund **des schlechten Wetters** wurde das Fußballspiel verschoben. *Due to the bad weather the football match was postponed.*	**Wessen?** *Whose?*

Normally there is only one nominative in one sentence. In sentences using the verbs **sein** *(to be)*, **heißen** *(to be called)*, **bleiben** *(to stay, remain)*, **werden** *(to become)*, however, due to their meaning, there can be more than one nominative.

Herr Richter **ist** ein guter Rechtsanwalt.	*Herr Richter is a good solicitor.*
Frau Latour **wird** sicher eine gute Juristin.	*Frau Latour is sure to become a good lawyer.*

Some verbs in German are always followed by the dative:
e.g. **antworten** *(to answer)*, **danken** *(to thank)*, **helfen** *(to help)*.

antworten	Frau Sanchez antwortet **dir**. *Frau Sanchez will answer you.*
helfen	Herr Graf hilft **der Verkaufsassistentin.** *Herr Graf is helping the sales assistant.*

It's best if you learn these by heart. In the appendix you'll find a list of all the "dative" verbs (p. 167ff.).

Other verbs can take both an accusative and a dative object just like in English! (In English we can also form the dative by adding "to"!)

bringen	Herr Lechner bringt **dem Vorstand die Folien**. *Herr Lechner takes the board members the transparencies.*
geben	Herr Mayer gibt **seinem Kollegen den Schlüssel**. *Herr Mayer gives his colleague the key.*

With these verbs the person is normally in the dative (**dem Vorstand, seinem Kollegen**) and the non-person or object in the accusative (**die Folien, den Schlüssel**). In the sentence the dative object always comes before the accusative object. If, however the accusative object is a pronoun, it comes first and the dative object second.

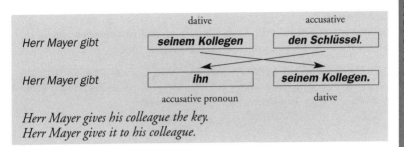

Herr Mayer gibt **seinem Kollegen** **den Schlüssel**.
dative · accusative

Herr Mayer gibt **ihn** **seinem Kollegen**.
accusative pronoun · dative

Herr Mayer gives his colleague the key.
Herr Mayer gives it to his colleague.

2.4 Die Deklination
Noun Declension
oder *Wer hilft dem Studenten?*

In forming the different cases, there are very few changes to the endings of the nouns themselves.

	singular masculine	neuter	feminine	plural
nom.	der Mann	das Kind	die Frau	die Leute
acc.	den Mann	das Kind	die Frau	die Leute
dat.	dem Mann	dem Kind	der Frau	den Leute**n**
gen.	des Mann**es**	des Kind**es**	der Frau	der Leute

For nouns in the singular the following is true:

- Feminine nouns remain the same in all cases.

- Masculine und neuter nouns in the genitive take the ending **-(e)s.**

- Nouns in the plural take an **-n** in the dative, unless they already end in **-n** or **-s:**

die Leute	mit den Leute**n**	*people, with the people*
die Frauen	mit den Frauen	*women, with the women*
die Autos	mit den Autos	*cars, with the cars*

Just to make things interesting, there are, of course, exceptions. Several masculine nouns belong to the so-called **n-declension**, where in all cases except the nominative singular **-(e)n** is added:

	type A	type B
nom.	der Student	der Name
acc.	den Student**en**	den Name**n**
dat.	dem Student**en**	dem Name**n**
gen.	des Student**en**	des Name**ns**
plural	die/den/der Student**en**	die/den/der Name**n**

Not to worry: only very few nouns behave like this and they are all masculine except for one: **Herz** *(heart)*: **das Herz** (nom. and acc.), **dem Herzen** (dat.), **des Herzens** (gen.).

■ Type A includes:

Male persons and animals that end in *-e*	
der Jung**e**	*boy*
der Kolleg**e**	*colleague*
der Franzos**e**	*Frenchman*
der Löw**e**	*lion*

Nouns that come from Latin or Greek ending in *-ant, -at, -ent, -ist*	
der Diam**ant**	*diamond*
der Demokr**at**	*democrat*
der Stud**ent**	*student*
der Optim**ist**	*optimist*

■ Type B includes:

A few abstract masculine nouns ending in *-e*	
der Fried**e**	*peace*
der Gedank**e**	*thought*
der Nam**e**	*name*

EXERCISE 4	Please complete the following nouns by adding the correct endings where necessary.

1. Die Verkäuferin half dem Kunde_____ bei der Suche.

2. Das ist mein Kollege_____ Martin.

3. Eine Redewendung besagt: Der Glaube_____ versetzt Berge.

4. Herr Techmer hilft dem Praktikant_____ bei der Seminararbeit.

5. Die Richterin glaubt dem Zeuge_____.

6. Die Journalistin interviewt einen Experte_____.

7. Ich muss mich bei dem Lieferant_____ beschweren.

8. Der Höhepunkt ist die Ansprache des Bundespräsident_____.

9. Die Fahndung nach dem Terrorist_____ läuft auf Hochtouren.

10. Darüber machten wir uns keine Gedanke_____.

3 Das Pronomen
Pronouns

oder

Ich, du und die anderen
Me, you and the others

Hallo, ich bin Alan, du bist sicher Eva, Peter hat mir schon viel von dir erzählt.

Hallo, Alan! Ja, ich bin Eva, und das hier ist Felix.

Ich wusste gar nicht, dass Peter einen Hund hat.

Das ist ja auch nicht sein Hund, sondern meiner.

Alan: Hello, I'm Alan. You must be Eva. Peter has told me so much about you.– Eva: Hello, Alan. Yes, I'm Eva. And this is Felix. – Alan: I didn't know that Peter had a dog. – Eva: Oh, it's not his dog, it's mine.

Pronouns are little words that often take the place of nouns or groups of nouns. They help us to avoid having to repeat things.

Milena kauft diesen Computer. **Sie** kauft **ihn**.	*Milena is buying this computer. She's buying it.*
Wem gehört diese Digitalkamera?	*Who does this digital camera belong to?*
Das ist **meine**.	*It's mine.*

Some pronouns, like the definite and indefinite articles (**bestimmter** und **unbestimmter Artikel**), can also accompany a noun. These pronouns are called **Possessivartikel** in German. They have the same function as possessive adjectives (**my, your, his** etc.) in English.

Das ist **mein** Handy.	*That's my mobile phone.*

These (adjectival) pronouns take on the gender, number and case of the noun that they stand for or describe.

3.1 Das Personalpronomen
Personal Pronouns
<u>oder</u> *Ich und du*

Personal pronouns represent the speaker or the person spoken to. They can also replace a person, a noun or a group of nouns. Depending on their role in the sentence their form reflects the appropriate grammatical case.

Ich lese den Bericht. (nom.)	*I'm reading the report.*
Möchtest **du** mit **uns** ins Kino gehen? (nom.; dat.)	*Would you like to go to the cinema with us?*
Der Assistent antwortet dem Abteilungsleiter.	*The assistant answers the head of department.*
Er antwortet **ihm**. (nom.; dat.)	*He answers him.*

singular	1st person	2nd person	3rd person masculine	neuter	feminine
nom.	*ich*	*du*	*er*	*es*	*sie*
acc.	*mich*	*dich*	*ihn*	*es*	*sie*
dat.	*mir*	*dir*	*ihm*	*ihm*	*ihr*
gen.	*(meiner)*	*(deiner)*	*(seiner)*	*(seiner)*	*(ihrer)*

plural	1st person	2nd person	3rd person	polite form
nom.	*wir*	*ihr*	*sie*	*Sie*
acc.	*uns*	*euch*	*sie*	*Sie*
dat.	*uns*	*euch*	*ihnen*	*Ihnen*
gen.	*(unser/ unserer)*	*(euer/ eurer)*	*(ihrer)*	*(Ihrer)*

We use the informal second person pronouns **du** (singular) and **ihr** (plural) when addressing children, good friends, family members or relations. Colleagues at work also often use the **du/ihr** form if they get on well together.

The formal second person pronoun **Sie** (both singular and plural) is used between strangers and adults who don't know each other well. It is also quite common for colleagues at work to use the **Sie** form even though they have known each other for years.

The formal and polite forms **Sie/Ihnen** remain the same in both the singular and the plural. They are always written with a capital letter.

The 3rd person singular pronoun has the same gender as the noun it stands for:

der: er	**Der Kollege** *raucht.* **Er** *raucht.*
	The colleague smokes. He smokes.
	Der Drucker *läuft.* **Er** *läuft.*
	The printer works. It works.

das: es	**Das Kind** weint. **Es** weint.
	The child is crying. He/She's crying.
	Das Telefon klingelt. **Es** klingelt.
	The telephone is ringing. It's ringing.

die: sie	**Die Chefin** kommt. **Sie** kommt.
	The boss is coming. She's coming.
	Die Tür geht auf. **Sie** geht auf.
	The door opens. It opens.

In the 3rd person plural no distinction in gender is necessary.
The genitive case of the personal pronouns is very rarely used.

EXERCISE 5 Please complete the following sentences
using the correct personal pronouns.

1. Mark arbeitet an einer neuen Homepage. Seit _____ sich mit Webdesign beschäftigt, sieht man _____ nur selten beim Joggen.
2. Julie sucht einen Job als Programmiererin. _____ hat auf diesem
   Gebiet bereits Erfahrungen gesammelt.
3. Carlos geht ein Jahr nach Deutschland, um seine Sprachkenntnisse
   zu verbessern. Es wird _____ dort bestimmt gefallen.
4. Hast _____ daran gedacht, dass Andrea heute eine Stelle als
   Praktikantin antritt? _____ solltest _____ viel Glück wünschen!
5. Herr Smith, ich danke _____, dass _____ gekommen sind. Ist
   _____ Frau auch dabei?
6. Elena hat noch verschiedene Prüfungen zu absolvieren. Wir werden
   _____ dabei helfen.
7. Andrew, soll ich _____ bei _____ Freundin abholen?
8. _____ werde _____ noch per E-Mail mit Frau Miller in Verbindung
   setzen.

3.2 Der Possessivartikel und das Possessivpronomen
Possessive Articles and Possessive Pronouns
oder *Alles meins!*

A possessive article indicates the person something belongs to:

Maria hat ein Handy. Sie hat **ihr** Handy immer dabei.	*Maria has got a mobile phone. She always has her mobile phone with her.*
Herr Romero sieht mit **seiner** neuen Brille besser aus als mit **seiner** alten.	*Herr Romero's new glasses suit him better than his old ones.*
Meine Kollegin und ich haben einen Bericht über die Konferenz angefertigt. **Unser** Bericht ist im Intranet abrufbar.	*My colleague and I have prepared a report on the conference. You can read our report on the intranet.*

The choice of possessive article is dictated by the person doing the possessing:

ich	*I*	**mein**	*my*
du	*you*	**dein**	*your*
Sie	*you,* formal	**Ihr**	*your*
er	*he*	**sein**	*his*
es	*it*	**sein**	*its*
sie	*she*	**ihr**	*her*
wir	*we*	**unser**	*our*
ihr	*you,* plural	**euer**	*your*
sie	*they*	**ihr**	*their*
Sie	*you,* plural, formal	**Ihr**	*your*

Possessive articles follow the same formal rules as the indefinite article and have the same endings depending on how the noun they refer to is used in the sentence:

*Das ist Simone und **ihr** Hund.*
(masculine, nom.)

That's Simone and her dog.

*Simone liebt **ihren** Hund.*
(masculine, acc.)

Simone loves her dog.

*Simone geht mit **ihrem** Hund
in die Arbeit.*
(masculine, dat.)

Simone goes to work with her dog.

There are two sides to every possessive article: the choice
and the ending. The choice is determined by the person or
the thing doing the possessing and the ending by the noun
and the role it plays in the sentence.

	singular			plural
	masculine	neuter	feminine	
nom.	*mein*	*mein*	*meine*	*meine*
	Computer	*Handy*	*Kamera*	*Sachen*
acc.	*meinen*	*mein*	*meine*	*meine*
	Computer	*Handy*	*Kamera*	*Sachen*
dat.	*meinem*	*meinem*	*meiner*	*meinen*
	Computer	*Handy*	*Kamera*	*Sachen*
gen.	*meines*	*meines*	*meiner*	*meiner*
	Computers	*Handys*	*Kamera*	*Sachen*

Possessive pronouns on the other hand stand alone, i.e. they don't have a
noun following them in a sentence.

Wem gehört der Ohrring?
*Das ist **meiner**.*

Who does the earring belong to?
It's mine.

Sind das eure Folien?
*Nein, das sind nicht **unsre**.*

Are those your transparencies?
No, they're not ours.

Possessive pronouns are declined in the same way as the definite article. They have the same endings (see 1.2, p. 17):

	singular			plural
	masculine	neuter	feminine	
	der Wagen	**das Haus**	**die Yacht**	**die Sachen**
nom.	*mein*er	*mein(e)*s	*mein*e	*mein*e
acc.	*mein*en	*mein(e)*s	*mein*e	*mein*e
dat.	*mein*em	*mein*em	*mein*er	*mein*en

Deiner, seiner and *ihrer* are declined in the same way. Instead of *unserer, unseres, unsere, euerer* you'll often find *unsrer, unsres, unsre, eurer.* Possessive pronouns in the genitive are no longer used in normal speech.

There are several other pronouns that behave in the same way, i.e. they can stand alone without a noun and have the same endings as the definite article: *irgendeiner, (irgend)welcher, jeder, (k)einer, mancher.*

3.3 Das Demonstrativpronomen
Demonstrative Pronouns
oder Dieses Buch

Demonstrative pronouns (*Demonstrativpronomen*) "demonstrate" whether something is here or there.

Dieses Briefing hier ist sehr informativ.	*This briefing is very informative.*
Diese Bewerbung ist die interessanteste von allen.	*This job-application is the most interesting of all.*

The following words can be used as demonstrative pronouns in German: *der, das, die (this/that); dieser (this); jener (that); solcher (such); derjenige (the one); derselbe (the same).*

In spoken language common use is made of the definite article as a demonstrative pronoun:

Welches Auto gefällt dir am besten? **Das** *hier.*	*Which car do you like best? This on here.*
Kennst du den Kollegen da drüben? Ja, **den** *kenne ich.*	*Do you know that colleague over there? Yes, I know him.*
Welches ist deine Tasse? **Die** *da.*	*Which is your cup? That one there.*

■ The forms are the same as those of the definite article except for the dative plural **denen** and the genitive: **dessen** (masculine + neuter), **derer** (feminine + plural).

■ The endings of the demonstrative pronouns **dieser, jener, solcher** are the same those of the definite article:

	masculine	neuter	feminine	plural
nom.	*dieser*	*dieses*	*diese*	*diese*
acc.	*diesen*	*dieses*	*diese*	*diese*
dat.	*diesem*	*diesem*	*dieser*	*diesen*
gen.	*dieses*	*dieses*	*dieser*	*dieser*

■ Both **derjenige** and **derselbe** are words with two halves. The first half follows the same rules as the definite article. The second half **-jenige** or **-selbe** remains the same in five instances, otherwise **-n** is added.

	masculine	neuter	feminine	plural
nom.	*derjenige*	*dasjenige*	*diejenige*	*diejenigen*
acc.	*denjenigen*	*dasjenige*	*diejenige*	*diejenigen*
dat.	*demjenigen*	*demjenigen*	*derjenigen*	*denjenigen*
gen.	*desjenigen*	*desjenigen*	*derjenigen*	*derjenigen*

Diejenigen, die mit den Aufgaben fertig sind, können hinausgehen.	*Those of you who have finished the exercises can go out.*
Das war wieder **dasselbe** komische Geräusch wie gestern Abend.	*That was the same funny noise as yesterday evening.*
Warum hörst du immer **dieselbe** Musik?	*Why do you always listen to the same music?*

EXERCISE 6a Please complete the following sentences with the correct demonstrative pronouns *dieser, dieses, diesem* and *diesen.*

1. Wer hat _____ Film mit Julia Roberts gesehen?
2. _____ CD-Player gehört Luca.
3. Wir wussten nicht, wie _____ Diktiergerät funktionierte.
4. _____ Verhalten gab mir zu denken.
5. Sie sollten _____ Vorfall keine Beachtung schenken.
6. Ich habe _____ Wort noch nie gehört.
7. _____ Fragen wurden mit Hilfe des Internets gelöst.
8. Carla wird _____ Wohnung in Hamburg mieten.

EXERCISE 6b Please put in the missing demonstrative pronouns.

Wir suchen Möbel für unsere Wohnung in Deutschland und finden in einem Einrichtungshaus …

1. … einen Küchentisch. – _____ ist leider zu groß für unsere Küche.
2. … einen Einbauschrank. – _____ gefällt uns ausgezeichnet.
3. … eine Eckbank. – _____ ist uns zu teuer.
4. … Stühle für die Essecke. – _____ können wir auf jeden Fall gebrauchen.
5. … einen Schreibtisch. – _____ ist etwas zu klein.
6. … eine Wohnzimmerlampe. – _____ sollten wir gleich mitnehmen.

3.4 Das Fragepronomen
Interrogative Pronouns
oder *Wer denn, wo denn, was denn?*

What kind of pronouns do we use when asking questions? Look at the following examples and the words in bold print:

Wer hat angerufen? *Who called?*	**Dr. Dorsch** hat gestern angerufen. *Dr. Dorsch called yesterday.*
Wen hast du getroffen? *Who did you meet?*	Ich habe gestern **Frau Richter** getroffen. *I met Frau Richter yesterday.*
Was steht in der E-Mail? *What was in the E-mail?*	In der E-Mail steht **der Liefertermin**. *The delivery date was in the Email.*

Using interrogative pronouns (or: w-question words) we can ask questions about different parts of a sentence. To ask about a person we use **wer?** and to ask about things we use **was?** They change their form according to case, depending on their grammatical role in the sentence.

	person	thing
nom.	wer?	was?
acc.	wen?	was?
dat.	wem?	was?
gen.	wessen?	wessen?

Interrogative pronouns are also used together with prepositions. Here, too, we have to distinguish between a person and a thing.

- If we ask about a person, then we use a preposition followed by the interrogative pronoun in the appropriate case.

An wen denkst du gerade? *Who are you thinking of?*	Ich denke an meinen Freund. *I'm thinking of my friend.*
Von wem spricht er? *Who is he talking about?*	Er spricht von seinem Kollegen. *He's talking about his colleague.*

■ If we ask about a thing, we use **wo(r)** + preposition.

Woran denkst du gerade? *What are you thinking of at the moment?*	Ich denke an meinen Urlaub. *I'm thinking of my holiday.*
Wovon erzählt er? *What's he talking about?*	Er erzählt von seinem Wochenend- ausflug. *He's talking about his weekend trip.*

Two more interrogative pronouns are **welcher** and **was für ein.** Just like possessive pronouns they can be used like an article with a noun or they can stand alone.

Welches Kleid gefällt dir am besten?	*Which dress do you like best?*
Hier sind verschiedene Kleider. **Welches** gefällt dir am besten?	*Here are several different dresses.* *Which do you like best?*
Was für eine Jacke suchst du?	*What kind of jacket are you looking for?*
Ich suche eine Lederjacke. **Was für eine** denn?	*I'm looking for a leather jacket.* *What kind of one then?*

Welcher, used either as an article or a pronoun, is declined in the same way. It takes the same signal endings as the definite article (see 1.2, p. 17). When using **was für einer,** remember that **was für** always remains the same and only **einer** changes.

Used as an article **einer** is declined in the same way as the indefinite article (see 1.2, p. 17). Used as a pronoun **einer** is declined in the same way as the definite article and takes the same signal endings (see 1.2, p. 17).

3.5 Das Reflexivpronomen und das Reziprokpronomen
Reflexive and Reciprocal Pronouns
oder *Ich freue mich...*

> Lieber Alan, ich freue mich sehr, dass du gekommen bist, Eva und Frank freuen sich auch, also wir freuen uns alle – trinken wir auf dein Wohl und auf eine schöne Zeit für dich hier in Deutschland.

Alan, I'm so glad you've come. Eva and Frank are glad, too. We're all very pleased. Here's to you and we hope you have a great time over here in Germany.

Here's some good news! Reflexive pronouns only occur in the accusative and dative. And apart from the 3rd person their forms are the same as the personal pronouns.

	accusative	dative
ich	**mich**	**mir**
du	**dich**	**dir**
er/es/sie	**sich**	**sich**
wir	**uns**	**uns**
ihr	**euch**	**euch**
sie/Sie	**sich**	**sich**

There are a large number of verbs in German that, unlike English, require a reflexive pronoun. They cannot stand alone. We call them reflexive verbs.

Er **bewirbt sich** um diese Stelle.	*He's applying for this job.*
Sie hat **sich** leider **erkältet.**	*Unfortunately she's caught a cold.*

 Always remember the reflexive pronoun when learning reflexive verbs (**sich bewerben, sich erkälten** …)!

There are other verbs that sometimes have a reflexive pronoun and sometimes don't, depending on their meaning.

Anne **wäscht** den Pullover.	*Anne is washing the pullover.*
Julian **wäscht sich** die Hände.	*Julian is washing his hands.*
Frau Böttcher **versteckt** das Geschenk.	*Frau Böttcher hides the present.*
Die Kinder **verstecken sich** im Schrank.	*The children hide in the cupboard.*

Reciprocal pronouns are used to express a "reciprocal" relationship between people or things. They correspond to the English *each other* or *one another.*

Harry Richter und Lisa Mayer **lieben sich** (oder: einander).	*Harry Richter and Lisa Mayer love each other.*
Die beiden Brüder **helfen sich** (gegenseitig).	*The two brothers help each other.*

The reciprocal pronoun **-einander** is used in combination with prepositions.

Die Akten liegen alle **übereinander**.	*The files are lying on top of one another.*
Heute Abend gehen die Team-mitglieder **miteinander** ins Improtheater.	*This evening the members of the team are accompanying each other to the Impro Theatre.*

EXERCISE 7   Please put in the correct reflexive and reciprocal pronouns.

1. Lars kauft _____ ein neues Sweatshirt.

2. Yukis Bemerkungen ärgerten _____.

3. Ich freue _____ über das bestandene Zertifikat.

4. Die Polizei interessierte _____ für den Vorfall.

5. Wir danken _____ beiden für die Einladung zur Party.

6. Frau Glück und Herr Wein helfen _____.

7. Alexander putzt _____ die Zähne.

8. Wir machten _____ über den Jahresabschluss Gedanken.

9. Die Kontoauszüge lagen durch_____ auf dem Tisch.

10. Heute gehen wir mit_____ ins Kino.

4 Das Adjektiv
Adjectives

oder

Sachen und Personen beschreiben
Describing things and people

Peter: You can have my old study. Since I've had this new job, I don't need it any more. It's not especially big unfortunately. – Alan: That really doesn't matter. I'm just happy that I can stay with a good friend while I do my work-experience programme. My room at home was even smaller and it didn't have such a good view!

Adjectives are used to describe, characterise or modify people and things – in grammatical terms they qualify nouns.

4.1 Die Adjektivendungen
Adjectival Endings
oder *Ende gut, alles gut*

Adjectives are easiest to use in German when they come after the noun because they remain in their basic form and don't change their endings.

Das Zimmer ist **schön**.	*The room is nice.*
Der Diskjockey ist **jung**.	*The disc jockey is young.*

Things become much more interesting, however, when the adjective comes in front of the noun. Here it takes on different endings: it has to be declined.

Herr Radwan bestellt einen französisch**en** Wein.	*Herr Radwan orders some wine from France.*
Der französisch**e** Wein schmeckt ihm.	*The wine from France tastes good.*
Frau Radwan isst Apfelstrudel mit heiß**er** Vanillesoße.	*Frau Radwan is eating apple strudel with hot custard.*

It's not too difficult to get the endings for the adjective right. They are determined by

- the article in front of the adjective and its signal ending
- the gender, number and case of the noun that follows

The following table will help you to remember.

> *der trockene Wein* *the dry wine*
> article **with** signal ending
> noun: masculine, singular, nom.
>
> *ein trockener Wein* *a dry wine*
> article **without** signal ending
> noun: masculine, singular, nom.

Now there are just two more rules for us to learn:

■ If the adjective is preceded by an article with a signal ending, then the adjective takes the ending **-e** oder **-en** (*der trockene Wein*).

	masculine	neuter	feminine	plural
nom.	-e	-e	-e	-en
acc.	-en	-e	-e	-en
dat.	-en	-en	-en	-en
gen.	-en	-en	-en	-en

■ If the adjective is preceded by an article without a signal ending (see 1.2, p. 17) or if there is no article at all, then the adjective itself is required to provide the necessary signal ending. Usually an **-e-** is added between the basic form of the adjective and the signal ending: *trockener Wein*.

To remind you, here again is a list of the signal endings:

	masculine	neuter	feminine	plural
nom.	r	s	e	e
acc.	n	s	e	e
dat.	m	m	r	n
gen.	s	s	r	r

In context the result is as follows:

	masculine	neuter	feminine	plural
nom.	der trockene Wein	das kühle Bier	die warme Milch	die guten Getränke
nom.	ein trockener Wein	ein kühles Bier	eine warme Milch	gute Getränke
nom.	trockener Wein	kühles Bier	warme Milch	gute Getränke
acc.	den trockenen Wein	das kühle Bier	die warme Milch	die guten Getränke
acc.	einen trockenen Wein	ein kühles Bier	eine warme Milch	gute Getränke
acc.	trockenen Wein	kühles Bier	warme Milch	gute Getränke
dat.	dem trockenen Wein	dem kühlen Bier	der warmen Milch	den guten Getränken
dat.	einem trockenen Wein	einem kühlen Bier	einer warmen Milch	guten Getränken
dat.	trockenem Wein	kühlem Bier	warmer Milch	guten Getränken
gen.	des trockenen Weines	des kühlen Bieres	der warmen Milch	der guten Getränke
gen.	eines trockenen Weines	eines kühlen Bieres	einer warmen Milch	guter Getränke
gen.	trockenen Weines	kühlen Bieres	warmer Milch	guter Getränke

The table shows how the signal endings can jump, as it were, between article and adjective.

The endings in the genitive masculine and neuter without an article are an exception. They differ from the expected signal endings and have **-en** instead. The signal ending jumps over to the noun. These forms do not occur very often though.

The two adjectives **lila** and **rosa** don't take any kind of ending:

Sie trägt eine **rosa** Bluse mit **lila** Streifen.	*She's wearing a pink blouse with purple stripes.*

EXERCISE 8   Please complete the following sentences by adding the correct endings to the adjectives.

1. Mit diesem Management wird das Unternehmen nie auf einen grün____ Zweig kommen.
2. Alicée will immer die erst__ Geige spielen.
3. Maria ist gerade noch einmal mit einem blau____ Auge davongekommen.
4. Hier geht doch etwas nicht mit recht____ Dingen zu.
5. Wir sollten das nicht an die groß__ Glocke hängen.
6. Mike wurde mit offen____ Armen empfangen.
7. An dieser Aufführung hat der Theaterkritiker kein gut____ Haar gelassen.
8. Mit diesem Vorhaben hast du dir kalt__ Füße geholt.
9. Das Ereignis traf uns wie ein Blitz aus heiter____ Himmel!
10. Dies sollte man nicht auf die leicht__ Schulter nehmen.

Each of these sentences contains a very useful idiomatic phrase for you to learn by heart. The translation can be found with the answer key in the appendix.

4.2 Die Steigerung des Adjektivs
The Comparison of the Adjective
oder *Schnell, schneller, am schnellsten*

In this age of rapid change and fierce competition the need to compare things has grown. In grammatical terms we can do this by using the positive (**Positiv**), comparative (**Komparativ**) and superlative (**Superlativ**) forms of the adjective.

■ Positive:

Das Mofa ist schnell.	The moped is fast.
Mein Motorrad ist so schnell wie deins.	My motorbike is as fast as yours.
Das schnelle Mofa gehört diesem Jungen.	The fast moped belongs to his boy.

■ Comparative: **+ -er**

Das Motorrad ist schneller als das Mofa.	The motorbike is faster than the moped.
Das schnellere Motorrad hat gewonnen.	The faster motorbike has won.

■ Superlative: **+ (e)sten**

Das Flugzeug ist am schnellsten.	The aeroplane is fastest.
Wir fliegen im schnellsten Flugzeug der Welt.	We're flying in the fastest aeroplane in the world.

When do adjectives in the comparative and superlative have different adjectival endings and when don't they? The same rules apply as for the normal form.

■ If the adjective comes after the noun, then it doesn't change:

Das Motorrad ist schneller als das Mofa.	The motorbike is faster than the moped.
Das Flugzeug ist am schnellsten.	The aeroplane is fastest.

■ The adjective takes on different endings if it comes in front of the noun:

Das schnellere Motorrad hat gewonnen.	The faster motorbike has won.
Wir fliegen im schnellsten Flugzeug der Welt.	We're flying in the fastest aeroplane in the world.

All three forms (positive, comparative and superlative) can come before or after the noun and they all obey the same rules as far as the correct endings are concerned.

■ There are, however, one or two special cases. The ending in the superlative is **-esten** if the adjective ends with **-d, -s, -ss, -ß, -sch, -t, -tz, -x, or -z** and the emphasis is on the final syllable:

gesund	gesünder	am gesünd**esten**
healthy	*healthier*	*healthiest*
schlecht	schlechter	am schlecht**esten**
bad	*worse*	*worst*
hübsch	hübscher	am hübsch**esten**
pretty	*prettier*	*prettiest*
stolz	stolzer	am stolz**esten**
proud	*prouder*	*proudest*

■ In lots of cases **a, o, u** change to **ä, ö, ü**, e.g.:

kalt	k**ä**lter	am k**ä**ltesten
cold	*colder*	*coldest*
groß	gr**ö**ßer	am gr**ö**ßten
big	*bigger*	*biggest*
klug	kl**ü**ger	am kl**ü**gsten
clever	*cleverer*	*cleverest*

■ Other irregular forms are:

gut	besser	am besten
good	*better*	*best*
viel	mehr	am meisten
much	*more*	*most*
hoch	höher	am höchsten
high	*higher*	*highest*
nah	näher	am nächsten
near	*nearer*	*nearest*

teuer	teurer	am teuersten
dear	*dearer*	*dearest*
dunkel	dunkler	am dunkelsten
dark	*darker*	*darkest*

The comparison of adjectives in German is easier than in English. Comparative and superlative are always formed in a similar way for all adjectives.

E X E R C I S E   9 | **Please complete the following sentences with the correct form of the adjective: positive, comparative or superlative.**

1. *groß:*

   Eileen ist so ＿＿＿＿＿＿ wie Pia.

   Pia ist ＿＿＿＿＿＿ als Marcus.

   Tom ist von allen Praktikanten ＿＿＿＿＿＿.

2. *gut:*

   Herr Porter spricht so ＿＿＿＿＿＿ Deutsch wie Frau Hundt.

   Frau Hundt spricht ＿＿＿＿＿＿ Deutsch als Sarah.

   Gina spricht ＿＿＿＿＿＿ Deutsch.

3. *gesund:*

   Limonade ohne Zucker ist ＿＿＿＿＿＿.

   Apfelschorle ist allerdings ＿＿＿＿＿＿.

   Und ein Glas Wein am Abend ist ＿＿＿＿＿＿.

4. *viel:*

   Über naturwissenschaftliche Erkenntnisse wusste Inka ＿＿＿＿＿＿.

   Über technische Neuerungen noch ＿＿＿＿＿＿.

   Und über sprachliche Angelegenheiten ＿＿＿＿＿＿.

5 Die Adverbien und Modalpartikel
Adverbs and Modal Particles

oder

Handlungen beschreiben
Describing Actions

Eva: Right, well I'll go home now then. You two men are sure to have
a lot to talk about and Alan probably wants to unpack still. –
Alan: Yes, quite. I have to go to work tomorrow. Do you live far away? –
Eva: No, I live just over there.

5.1 Adverbien
Adverbs
oder *Es kommt auf das Wie an*

Adverbs (**Adverbien**) describe how, where, when, where to, where from, how long or why something happens. But don't worry too much. Here is some good news for you: Adverbs never need to be declined! And apart from that, many adverbs have the same form as adjectives and the same comparative and superlative forms as well.

■ Adverbs of Location/Place

draußen	*Bei diesem schönen Wetter essen wir **draußen**.*
outside	*The weather is so nice we can eat outside.*
nirgends	*Ich kann meine Brille **nirgends** finden.*
nowhere/	*I can't find my glasses anywhere.*
not ... anywhere	

■ Adverbs of Direction

dahin	*Er läuft **dahin**.*
there/in that direction	*He's running there.*
hinauf	*Die Kinder klettern den Baum **hinauf**.*
up	*The children climb up the tree.*

■ Adverbs of Time

heute	***Heute** habe ich leider keine Zeit.*
today	*I don't have time today, I'm afraid.*
meistens	*Wenn Mona in die Stadt fährt, parkt sie **meistens** im Parkhaus.*
mostly/usually	*When Mona drives into town, she usually parks in the multi-storey carpark.*

■ Adverbs of Manner

leider	Frank kann **leider** nicht mit ins Konzert kommen.
unfortunately	*Frank can't come with us to the concert unfortunately.*
langsam	Es ist gesund, **langsam** zu essen.
slowly	*It's healthy to eat slowly.*

■ Adverbs of Cause

Adverbs of cause can be used as a replacement for conjunctions.

trotzdem	Es regnet. **Trotzdem** mache ich jetzt einen Spaziergang.
nevertheless	*It's raining. Nevertheless I'm going for a walk.*
deshalb	Marias Eltern wohnen in Kanada. **Deshalb** fliegt sie jedes Jahr dorthin.
for that reason	*Maria's parents live in Canada. She flies there every year for that reason.*

Adverbs form only a very small part of German grammar. They are no more than simple vocabulary items. Is that all we have to remember? Well, no. Not quite. There are a few irregular comparative and superlative forms that you need to learn. Here they are:

bald	eher	am ehesten
soon	*sooner*	*soonest*
gern	lieber	am liebsten
gladly	*rather/preferably*	*most of all*
oft	öfter/häufiger	am häufigsten
often	*more often*	*most often*
viel	mehr	am meisten
much	*more*	*most of all*

Where do we put adverbs in a sentence?

■ Directly after a verb:

*Sie singt **schön**.*   *She sings beautifully.*

■ Alongside a noun:

*Das Konzert **gestern** war fantastisch.*   *The concert yesterday was fantastic.*

■ Together with an adjective:

*Dieser Film ist **ziemlich** spannend.*   *The film is rather exciting.*

■ At the very beginning:

***Gestern** war das Konzert fantastisch.*
(for emphasis)   *Yesterday the concert was fantastic.*

Even whole phrases can be used as adverbs:

*Sie singt **schön**.*   *She sings beautifully.*
*Sie singt **hier**.*   *She's singing here.*
*Sie singt **in der Oper**.*   *She's singing in the opera.*

And what do we do when there are several adverbs or adverbial expressions in one sentence? Where do we put them all? In what order or sequence? A useful rule of thumb is: Time – Cause – Manner and Location/Place. But if a certain part of the sentence needs to be emphasised, then it can be placed elsewhere in a different order.

Er arbeitet heute (Time) wegen der kommenden Prüfung (Cause) fieberhaft (Manner) in der Bibliothek (Location/Place).
He's working today feverishly in the library because of the impending exam.

> *Wegen der kommenden Prüfung arbeitet er heute fieberhaft in der Bibliothek.*
> *Because of the impending exam he's working feverishly today in the library.*

 Think of a Tea-drinking CaMeL!

5.2 Die Modalpartikel
Modal Particles
oder *Aber eigentlich vielleicht doch...*

Modal particles (**Modalpartikel**) add a little spice to the language recipe. They aren't always strictly necessary, but they do give language a better flavour.

Modal particles are used for the most part in spoken language to express feelings, emotions and subjective views. The same particles used in different contexts and with different emphasis can have different meanings.

Da bist du **ja!**	*There you are!*
possible meanings:	
Ich freue mich, dass du da bist.	*I'm glad you're here.*
Ich ärgere mich, dass ich auf dich warten musste.	*I'm annoyed at having had to wait for you.*

Peter: Willst du mit ins Kino?	*Peter: Do you want to come to the cinema with me?*
Alan: **Eigentlich** müsste ich für meine Prüfung lernen.	*Alan: Actually, I ought to be studying for my exam.*
possible meanings:	
Ich habe keine Lust zu lernen, fühle mich aber verpflichtet.	*I don't really want to study, but I feel I must.*
Ich will lieber lernen, aber ich will dich auch nicht enttäuschen.	*I'd prefer to study, but I don't want to disappoint you.*

Was liest du **denn** da?	*What's that you're reading?*
possible meanings:	
Ich interessiere mich für das, was du liest.	*I'm interested in what you're reading.*
Ich ärgere mich darüber, dass du etwas liest, weil du etwas anderes tun solltest.	*I'm annoyed that you're reading when you should be doing something else.*

Here are some other modal particles in common use:

modal particle	example	possible meaning
aber	Das ist **aber** gut! *That's really good!*	You're surprised.
bloß	Was hast du denn **bloß**? *What ever is the matter?*	You're emphasising your feelings. Here: worry.
denn	Wie heißt du **denn**? *So what's your name?*	You're showing interest.
doch	Hier ist **doch** die Brille. *Your glasses are over here.*	You're emphasising something.
eben	Das ist **eben** das Leben. *That's life, isn't it?*	You're emphasising your feelings. Here: resignation.
etwa	Sind die Entwürfe **etwa** noch nicht fertig? *Don't tell me the designs aren't ready yet!*	You're showing amazement or annoyance.
halt	Hans ist **halt** so. *Hans just happens to be like that.*	You're emphasing your emotions. Here: resignation.
mal	Halte das bitte **mal** für mich. *Hold that for me a minute, would you?*	Friendly request.
nur	Ich wollte ja **nur** fragen. *I was only asking.*	You want to justify yourself.
schon	Das wird **schon** richtig sein so. *That'll be OK as it is.*	You confirm a previous statement and show no further interest.
wohl	Das Paket wird **wohl** morgen eingehen. *The parcel will arrive tomorrow, I expect.*	You're expressing an assumption.

The best way to learn modal particles is to learn them in context. Listen carefully to native speakers of German as much as possible and make a note of how they use these little words in everyday speech.

E X E R C I S E   1 0   **Please complete the following sentences using one of the modal particles in brackets.**

1. Das habe ich mir (denn / eben / nur) _____ vorgenommen.

2. Daran hat Vivian in der Eile (etwa / halt / mal) _____ nicht mehr gedacht.

3. Wo habe ich (bloß / aber / schon) _____ meine Uhr hingelegt?

4. Was ist (vielleicht / eben / denn) _____ hier los!

5. Das ist (wohl / aber / bloß) _____ großzügig von Ihnen!

6. Genau das habe ich (mal / etwa / doch) _____ gerade befürchtet!

7. Andy hat das (wohl / mal / etwa) _____ nicht so ernst genommen.

8. Dies konnte ich mir (eben / ja / bloß) _____ denken!

6 Die Wortstellung
The Word Order

oder

Sätze richtig bauen
Making correct sentences

Hallo, hier ist Alan, ich wollte nur sagen, dass ich gut angekommen bin ... Wie die Fahrt war? Na ja, etwas anstrengend ... Peter hat mich abgeholt und wir haben den Abend hier verbracht ... Und morgen beginnt schon das Praktikum.

Von hier ist es nicht weit bis in die Firma. Peter wird mich morgen mit dem Auto mitnehmen ...

Alan: Hello, it's Alan. I just wanted to let you know I've arrived ... What the journey was like? Oh, pretty tiring ... Peter picked me up and we spent the evening here ... And my work programme starts tomorrow. – It's not far from here to the office. Peter's taking me with him tomorrow in his car ...

Word order in German is, generally speaking, just as liberal as in English – and even more so sometimes. But there are one or two rules that are uniquely German.

The most important of these is the position of the verb or verbs in a sentence. The word order varies depending on whether you're forming a statement, a question with an interrogative pronoun, a question without an interrogative pronoun, an imperative or a subordinate clause.

■ Statement *(Aussagesatz)*

Er **liest** das Protokoll.	*He's reading the minutes.*

■ Question with Interrogative Pronoun *(Fragesatz mit Fragewort)*

Was **liest** er?	*What is he reading?*

■ Question without Interrogative Pronoun *(Fragesatz ohne Fragewort)*

Liest er wirklich das Protokoll?	*Is he really reading the minutes?*

■ Imperative *(Imperativ)*

Kommen Sie bitte sofort!	*Please come at once.*

■ Subordinate Clause *(Nebensatz)*

Ich weiß, dass er das Protokoll **liest**.	*I know that he's reading the minutes.*

In statements, the main inflected verb always comes in second place. The subject is placed as close as possible to the verb, either immediately before or after it. If there are several verbs in the sentence or uninflected parts of verbs like infinitives or participles, these always go to the end, thus forming a kind of verbal bracket around the rest of the sentence.

position 1	position 2 (inflected verb)	middle (variable number of elements)	end (other verbs or parts of verbs)
Alan	**beginnt**	heute sein Praktikum bei BMW in München.	
Heute	**beginnt**	Alan sein Praktikum bei BMW in München.	
Wann	**beginnt**	Alan sein Praktikum bei BMW in München?	
Heute	**fängt**	das Praktikum von Alan bei BMW in München	**an.**
Gestern	**hat**	das Praktikum von Alan bei BMW in München	**angefangen.**
Wo	**hat**	Alan gestern ein Praktikum	**angefangen?**
Alan	**hätte**	gestern sein Praktikum bei BMW in München	**anfangen sollen.**

Alan begins his work programme today at BMW in Munich.

Today Alan begins his work programme at BMW in Munich.

When does Alan begin his work programme at BMW in Munich?

Today Alan's work programme at BMW in Munich starts.

Yesterday Alan's work programme at BMW in Munich started.

Where did Alan start his work programme yesterday?

Alan should have started his work programme at BMW in Munich yesterday.

In questions, on the other hand, the sentence starts immediately with the verb:

inflected verb	middle	end (other verbs or parts of verbs)
Fängst	du morgen dein Praktikum	an?
Hat	dein Praktikum schon	begonnen?
Gehst	du mit uns heute Abend ins Kino?	

Are you starting your work programme tomorrow?
Has your work programme already started?
Are you going to the cinema with us this evening?

In subordinate clauses (Nebensätzen) all verbs and parts of verbs come at the end:

main clause	subordinate clause	verbs in the subordinate clause	main clause
Ich freue mich,	dass du	**gekommen bist.**	
	Weil du Filme so	**magst,**	wollten wir dich heute Abend ins Kino einladen.
Er fragt sich,	welches Handy er	**kaufen soll.**	
	Sobald ich	**angekommen bin,**	werde ich euch anrufen.

I'm glad you've come.
Because you like films so much, we wanted to invite you to come with us to the cinema this evening.
He's wondering which mobile phone he should buy.
As soon as I've arrived, I'll call you.

If the main clause follows the subordinate clause, then it starts immediately with the verb since the subordinate clause has taken over first position in the sentence instead of the main clause.

position 1	position 2 (inflected verb)	middle	end (other parts of verbs)
Sobald ich angekommen bin,	werde	ich euch	anrufen.
As soon as I've arrived, I'll call you.			

Now you know the most important rules about word order in German sentences. The various elements in the middle part of a sentence can be ordered in different ways. You'll learn about these in each individual chapter of this book (see 2.3 on p. 30ff., 5.1 on p. 59ff.).

EXERCISE 11a — Please change the word order in the following sentences and start with the part in bold print.

1. Hardy hat **am Montag** eine Agenda für das nächste Meeting erhalten.
2. Rebecca hat dieses Geschenk **von ihrem Mann** bekommen.
3. Die Touristen nehmen **um 10.30 Uhr** an einer Stadtführung teil.
4. Yvonne hat **heute** einen Termin in der Autowerkstatt.
5. Frau Simon hätte **den Gesprächstermin** wahrnehmen sollen.
6. Margarita fährt **mit dem Bus** in die Stadt.

EXERCISE 11b — Please turn the following statements into questions.

1. Ich gehe heute Abend mit Muriel in die Stadt.
2. Wir besuchen am Wochenende meine Cousine.
3. Am Samstag muss ich mich auf das Bewerbungsgespräch vorbereiten.
4. Wir treffen uns heute Nachmittag auf eine Tasse Kaffee.
5. Ich beschäftige mich gerade mit den Regeln der deutschen Grammatik.
6. Das Training hat bereits begonnen.

7 Die Verben
Verbs

oder

Was so alles passiert
Things that happen

Dieser Schreibtisch da drüben ist Ihr fester Arbeitsplatz. Natürlich werden Sie im Laufe des Praktikums auch tageweise in anderen Abteilungen sein, aber hier haben Sie sozusagen ihr Zuhause.

Wunderbar, dann kann's ja gleich losgehen.

Langsam, langsam. Bevor Sie sich in die Arbeit stürzen, führt Frau Huber Sie erst mal durch die Firma, damit Sie alles kennen lernen. Danach melden Sie sich wieder bei mir ...

Herr Schmidt: That desk over there will be your main place of work. Of course, while you're here you'll also be in other departments on a day-to-day basis, but here you'll have your home base, so to speak. – Alan: Great, when can we get started? – Herr Schmidt: Not so fast. Before you rush into things, Frau Huber will show you around the firm so you can get to know things. After that come back and see me ...

We are now going to take you on a journey through the wonderful world of verbs, a story with many chapters. In German, verbs play an especially important role in a variety of ways. On the one hand, just as in English, they define and provide meaning to an important part of any sentence: verbs tell us what someone does or what happens. In a grammatical sense the verb is king: it always takes up a specially reserved position in the sentence (see p. 67ff.) and it "rules" by determining the case of the nouns (see 2.3, p. 30ff.).

Verbs, too, can change their form (conjugation). They change according to:

■ Person

> *ich lese; du liest; er liest; wir lesen*
> *I read; you read; he reads; we read*

■ Tense

> *ich lese heute; ich las gestern ...*
> *I am reading today; I was reading yesterday ...*

■ Mood (Indicative/Subjunctive)

> *ich lese (wirklich); ich lese jetzt nicht, aber ich würde (gerne) lesen*
> *I am (actually) reading; I am not reading now, but I would (like to) read*

■ Voice (Active/Passive)

> *Ich lese diese Fachzeitschrift jede Woche.*
> *I read this magazine every week.*
>
> *Diese Fachzeitschrift wird von vielen gelesen.*
> *This magazine is read by many people.*

Fortunately the different forms can often be recognized by the endings that are added to the main verb stem depending on the person. These endings are as follows:

regular endings	
ich	–
du	**-st**
er/es/sie	–
wir	**-en**
ihr	**-t**
sie/Sie	**-en**

In the present indicative the ending for **ich** (singular) is: **-e** and the ending for **er, es, sie** is **-t.** Exceptions are the modal verbs and the verb **sein** *(to be)*.

Here are two examples:

	simple past	present
ich	schrieb- –	schreib-**e**
du	schrieb-**st**	schreib-**st**
er/es/sie	schrieb- –	schreib-**t**
wir	schrieb-**en**	schreib-**en**
ihr	schrieb-**t**	schreib-**t**
sie/Sie	schrieb-**en**	schreib-**en**
	stem + ending	stem + ending

Two identical sounds are combined into one.
E.g.: *wir sagt-te-en* becomes **sag-te-n**
(first person plural simple past).

The basic form of the verb, the infinitive, never changes and always ends in **-en: schreiben** *(to write)*, **sagen** *(to say)*, **wissen** *(to know)*. Exception: **sein** *(to be)*

There are, however, several quite different types of verbs in German … but let's not rush things. We'll deal with them all in turn.

7.1 Die Hilfsverben
Auxiliary Verbs
oder *Sein, haben und werden*

The three verbs **sein, haben** and **werden** can either be independent main verbs in their own right, or they can help out other verbs in an auxiliary function to form the different tenses of those verbs:

Vanessa **hat** Boxhandschuhe. = **haben** as a main verb	*Vanessa has some boxing-gloves.*
Vanessa **hat** Boxhandschuhe **gekauft.** = **haben** as an auxiliary forming the perfect tense of **kaufen**	*Vanessa has bought some boxing-gloves.*
Herr Gabor **ist** Rechtsanwalt. = **sein** as a main verb	*Herr Gabor is a solicitor.*
Herr Vollmer **ist** zu einem Rechtsanwalt **gegangen**. = **sein** as an auxiliary forming the perfect tense of **gehen**	*Herr Vollmer has gone to a solicitor.*
Carmen **wird** Informatikerin. = **werden** as a main verb	*Carmen is about to become a computer expert.*
Die Datei **wird gespeichert**. = **werden** as an auxiliary forming the present tense passive of **speichern**	*The file is being stored.*

These three verbs are exceptional also in the way they are conjugated. Their present tense forms are as follows:

	sein	haben	werden
ich	**bin**	hab-**e**	werd-**e**
du	**bi-st**	ha-**st**	wir-**st**
er/es/sie	**is-t**	ha-**t**	wir-**d**
wir	**sind**	hab-**en**	werd-**en**
ihr	**seid**	hab-**t**	werd-**et**
sie/Sie	**sind**	hab-**en**	werd-**en**

Remember that in German there are no continuous or progressive forms of the verb. Unlike English, the continuous aspect can be expressed by the normal "simple" form. The translations given here reflect this, depending on the meaning and the context.

7.2 Die Modalverben
Modal Verbs
<u>oder</u> *Müsste ich eigentlich können*

> Guten Tag, ich bin Alan und möchte mich für einen Deutschkurs anmelden.

> Dazu müssen Sie bitte dieses Formular ausfüllen. Wollen Sie einen Ganztags-, einen Halbtags- oder einen Abendkurs besuchen?

> Ich kann leider nur abends kommen, weil ich tagsüber arbeiten muss. Ich kann schon relativ gut Deutsch und möchte hauptsächlich meine Grammatik und meinen schriftlichen Ausdruck verbessern.

> Dann dürfte wahrscheinlich der Dienstagabendkurs für Sie passend sein, aber genau können wir das erst sagen, wenn Sie den Einstufungstest gemacht haben.

Alan: Hello, I'm Alan and I'd like to register for a German course. –
Secretary: You'll have to fill in this form then, please. Do you want to take a full-day, a half-day or an evening course? – Alan: I can only come in the evenings unfortunately because I have to go to work during the day.
I can already speak German quite well and I'd really like to improve my grammar and written work. – Secretary: Then the Tuesday evening course should suit you best, but we can only say for certain when you've done our assessment test.

Modal verbs are normally used in combination with the infinitive of a main verb. They describe the way or the manner in which things happen and often reflect the personal attitude or perspective of the speaker. One and the same modal verb can often have a variety of meanings as a result.

Sie **kann** sehr schön **singen**.	*She can sing most beautifully.* = ability
Kannst du mir mal **helfen**?	*Can you help me?* = friendly request
Hier **darf** man nicht **rauchen**.	*You're not allowed to smoke here.* = (no) permission
Er **muss** den Bericht heute Abend abgeben.	*He's got to deliver the report this evening.* = obligation

In the following table you can see the various meanings modal verbs can have:

dürfen	permission	Sie **dürfen** hier parken.	*You can/may park here.*
	politeness	**Darf** ich Ihnen meinen neuen Assistenten vorstellen?	*May I introduce my new assistent?*
	presumption	Die Besprechung **dürfte** um 10 Uhr beendet sein.	*The meeting should be over at 10 o'clock.*
nicht dürfen	permission denied	In der Kantine **darf** man nicht rauchen.	*You are not allowed to smoke in the cantine.*

können	friendly request	**Können** Sie mich mit Frau Aristov verbinden?	*Can you put me through to Frau Aristov?*
	possibility	Herr Bari hat Zeit und **kann** Frau Kundera vom Flughafen abholen.	*Herr Bari has got time and can pick up Frau Kundera from the airport.*
	ability	Oliver **kann** problemlos einen Marathon laufen.	*Oliver can run the marathon without any problem.*
	permission	Sie **können** den Dienstwagen nehmen.	*You can take the firm's car.*
mögen	to like/love	Linda **mag** Schoko-ladeneis.	*Linda likes chocolate ice cream.*
„möchte"	wish	Paula **möchte** einmal nach Südafrika reisen.	*Paula would like to travel to South Africa.*
	politeness	Ich **möchte** gerne mit Herrn Schmidt sprechen.	*I'd like to speak to Herr Schmidt, please.*
müssen	obligation, instruction, necessity	Wir **müssen** das Exposé bis Montag abgeben.	*We must deliver the exposé by Monday.*
		Sie **müssen** sich zuerst an der Pforte melden.	*You'll have to check in at the front door.*
sollen	indirect command, instruction	Herr Baumann hat gesagt, Sie **sollen** ihn zurückrufen.	*Herr Baumann said you were to call him back.*
wollen	will, intention, aim	Wir **wollen** uns in diesem Marktsegment neu positionieren.	*We want to establish a new position for ourselves in this market segment.*

The word **möchte** is often used in spoken language. It's a form of the verb **mögen** and has no infinitive form of its own.

The following table shows all the present tense forms of the modal verbs:

	dürfen	können	müssen	wollen	mögen		sollen
ich	darf	kann	muss	will	mag	möcht-e	soll
du	darf-st	kann-st	muss-t	will-st	mag-st	möcht-e-st	soll-st
er/es/ sie	darf	kann	muss	will	mag	möcht-e	soll
wir	dürf-en	könn-en	müss-en	woll-en	mög-en	möcht-en	soll-en
ihr	dürf-t	könn-t	müss-t	woll-t	mög-t	möcht-et	soll-t
sie/Sie	dürf-en	könn-en	müss-en	woll-en	mög-en	möcht-en	soll-en

 Apart from **möchte** and **sollen** all the modal verbs change their main vowel in the singular.
The verb **brauchen** can be used with **nur** or **nicht** like a modal verb and then takes on the same meaning as **müssen**. The infinitive is then formed with **zu**.

Du **brauchst** mir das nicht auf**zu**schreiben, ich kann es mir so merken.	*You don't have to write it down for me, I can remember it without.*
Du **musst** mir das nicht aufschreiben, ich kann es mir so merken.	*You don't have to write it down for me, I can remember it without.*

Sometimes modal verbs can be used on their own without another main verb or infinitive:

Ich **will** ein Eis.	*I want an ice cream.*
Sie **kann** das.	*She can do it.*
Ihr **dürft** das.	*You may (do that).*

EXERCISE 12   Please complete the following sentences with the correct modal verb.

1. _____ Andrew Deutsch sprechen? – Ja, er _____ aber seine Kenntnisse noch erweitern.

2. _____ du heute noch lernen? – Ja, ich _____!

3. Ich _____ Ihnen doch bestimmt eine kleine Erfrischung anbieten, oder ...? – Ja, Sie _____.

4. Bitte beachten Sie, dass Sie auf Bahnhöfen nicht rauchen _____.

5. An dieser Stelle _____ Sie nicht parken.

6. Du _____ mit mir noch einige Worte sprechen?

7. Über das Jobsharing _____ wir uns nochmals Gedanken machen.

8. Hier _____ Sie leise sein.

7.3   Die Verben mit Präfix
Verbs with a Prefix
oder Durchlesen, verstehen und wiedergeben

In German, lots of verbs can be combined with prefixes to form new verbs with different meanings.
If these prefixes are separable, then they also take the main stress when spoken.

■ Separable prefixes are:

| **ab-** | abholen | Peter **holt** Herrn Sailer vom Flughafen **ab**. *Peter is picking Herr Sailer up from the airport.* |
| **an-** | anrufen | **Rufen** Sie mich nächste Woche wieder **an**. *Give me another call next week.* |

auf-	aufmachen	Warten Sie, ich **mache** Ihnen die Tür **auf**. *Wait a moment, I'll open the door for you.*
aus-	ausfüllen	**Füllen** Sie bitte dieses Formular **aus**. *Please fill in this form.*
ein-	einstellen	Zum 1.10. **stellen** wir zehn neue Leute **ein**. *We shall be employing ten new people on 1.10.*
(he)raus- **(he)rein-**	hereinkommen	**Kommen** Sie doch bitte **herein**! *Please do come in!*
her-	herstellen	Wir **stellen** optische Geräte **her**. *We manufacture optical equipment.*
hin-	hinfahren	In München ist eine Fachtagung. Da f**ahren** wir **hin**. *There's a conference in Munich. We're going there.*
mit-	mitbringen	Jeder **bringt** zur Besprechung neue Ideen **mit**. *Everyone will bring new ideas with them to the meeting.*
nach-	nachsehen	Ich **sehe** mal **nach**, ob Ihre Unterlagen schon fertig sind. *I'll just see if your documents are finished yet.*
vor-	vorstellen	Heute **stellen** sich die Bewerber für die Technikerstelle **vor**. *Today the applicants for the technician's job will be coming for an interview.*
weg-	weggehen	Herr Maier ist leider nicht da, er **geht** immer um vier Uhr **weg**. *Herr Maier isn't here unfortunately, he always leaves at four o'clock.*
weiter-	weiterleiten	Bitte **leiten** Sie diese Information an alle Abteilungsleiter **weiter**. *Please pass this information on to all heads of department.*

zu-	zuhören	Wir **hörten** alle gespannt **zu**.
		We all listened attentively.
zurück-	zurückkommen	Frau Bolden **kommt** erst morgen früh von ihrer Dienstreise **zurück**.
		Frau Bolden won't be back from her business trip until tomorrow morning.

Prefixes that are inseparable are not stressed when spoken. As their name suggests, they cannot stand alone.

■ Inseparable prefixes are:

be-	bearbeiten	Lydia **bearbeitet** die neue Produktbeschreibung.
		Lydia is working on the description of the new product.
emp-	empfehlen	Wir **empfehlen** die Vorteilspackung zu 1000 Stück.
		We recommend the economy pack of 1000.
ent-	entscheiden	Das **entscheidet** die Chefin.
		The boss will decide that.
er-	erschrecken	Diese Umsatzzahlen **erschrecken** die Aktionäre.
		These sales figures will frighten the shareholders.
ge-	gelingen	Die Überraschung ist dir wirklich **gelungen**.
		You've succeeded in surprising us.
miss-	missverstehen	Da haben Sie mich wohl **missverstanden**.
		You must have misunderstood me.
ver-	versuchen	Ich **versuche**, Frau Maiwald zu erreichen.
		I'm trying to get hold of Frau Maiwald.
zer-	zerbrechen	Die Vase ist in tausend Scherben **zerbrochen**.
		The vase broke into a thousand pieces.

Some prefixes may be both stressed and separable as well as unstressed and inseparable. In each case the verb of which they are part has a different meaning. These prefixes are **durch-, über-, unter-, um-**.

prefix	verb	separable, stressed	inseparable, unstressed
durch-	durchbrechen	Das dünne Eis **bricht** unter ihrem Gewicht **durch**. *The thin ice breaks under her weight.*	Die Globalisierungs-gegner **durchbrechen** die Polizeiabsperrung. *The opponents of globalisation break through the police barrier.*
über-	übersetzen	Wir **setzen** von Calais nach Dover **über**. *We're taking the ferry from Calais to Dover.*	Bitte **übersetzen** Sie diesen Text. *Please translate this text.*
unter-	untergehen	Es ist schon spät, die Sonne **geht** schon **unter**. *It's late, the sun is already setting.*	
	unterbrechen		Niemand **unterbrach** den Redner. *No-one interrupted the speaker.*
um-	umstellen	Wir **stellen** unser Produktsortiment völlig **um**. *We are changing our range of products completely.*	Der Bankräuber konnte nicht mehr fliehen – das Gebäude war **umstellt**. *The bankrobber couldn't escape – the building was surrounded.*

EXERCISE 13 Please fill in the correct separable and inseparable verbs.

1. verfallen: Durch die Euro-Einführung _____ bestimmte Briefmarken _____.
2. anfangen: Der Film „Harry Potter" _____ um 20.00 Uhr _____.
3. übersetzen: Herr Brown _____ den Text ins Deutsche _____.
4. umschreiben: Der Trainer _____ die unbekannte Vokabel mit Synonymen _____.
5. abgeben: Der Kurier _____ das Paket an der Pforte _____.
6. umziehen: Am Sonntag _____ Pamela in die neue Wohnung _____.
7. gefallen: Der Dom und die Steinerne Brücke in Regensburg _____ mir _____.
8. ausfallen: Das Training-on-the-Job _____ heute _____.
9. unterstellen: Dieses böswillige Verhalten _____ man Kim _____.
10. zerfallen: Die Tagesordnung _____ in acht umfangreiche Punkte _____.

7.4 Die Verben mit festen Präpositionen
Verbs with Fixed Prepositions
oder Wir freuen uns auf vieles

In German, in some ways very similar to English, there are lots of verbs that form a close relationship with certain prepositions. These prepositional verbs then take on another meaning of their own. The preposition becomes a fixed part of the verb phrase and defines the case of the noun that follows.

■ **sich freuen über** + accusative

Isabelle hat eine sehr gute Note bei der Prüfung bekommen.	*Isabelle got good marks in the exam.*
Sie **freut sich über** das Ergebnis.	*She is very pleased about the result.*

■ **sich freuen auf** + accusative

Isabelle **freut sich auf** ihr Praktikum nächsten Monat.	*Isabelle is looking forward to starting her work-experience programme next month.*

■ **einladen zu** + dative

Wir **laden** Sie **zur** Einweihung unserer neuen Firmenräume **ein.**	*We'd like to invite you to the official opening of our new offices.*

■ **sich entschuldigen bei** + dative,
  sich entschuldigen für + accusative

Herr Maiwald hat sich **bei** uns **für** die verspätete Lieferung **entschuldigt.**	*Herr Maiwald apologized to us for the late delivery.*

Always try to think of these prepositional verbs as single expressions and learn them as one item, e.g.: **denken an** + accusative. In the appendix (p. 170ff.) you'll find a list of the most important ones.

8 Das Präsens und der Imperativ
The Present Tense and the Imperative
oder
Wie man fast alles sagen kann
How to say almost anything

Now run! Come on! Shoot, lad, shoot! Yes, that's a good pass, keep it up now! Come on, lads, show them! We're leading 1 : 0, we're going to win.

Just as football is more than just a sport to lots of people, the present tense in German is more than just a way of expressing present time. It can be used almost universally.

But first let's look at the various forms of the verb in the present tense.

8.1 Formen des Präsens
Forms of the Present Tense
oder *Starke und schwache Verben*

To form the present tense correctly you have to remember two things:

- Firstly, the correct ending: formed by removing the **-en** from the end of the infinitive and replacing it with the ending appropriate to the person (see 7, p. 73).

- Secondly, you have to know whether you are dealing with a weak (or regular) verb – in which case the verb stem remains the same for all persons. Irregular verbs (also called strong verbs), on the other hand, undergo a vowel change in the main stem and sometimes change the stem completely. Fortunately this happens only in the 2nd and 3rd person singular.

	wohnen *(regular)*	arbeiten *(regular)*	fahren *(irregular)*	nehmen *(irregular)*
ich	wohn-**e**	arbeit-**e**	fahr-**e**	nehm-**e**
du	wohn-**st**	arbeit-**est**	fähr-**st**	nimm-**st**
er/es/sie	wohn-**t**	arbeit-**et**	fähr-**t**	nimm-**t**
wir	wohn-**en**	arbeit-**en**	fahr-**en**	nehm-**en**
ihr	wohn-**t**	arbeit-**et**	fahr-**t**	nehm-**t**
sie/Sie	wohn-**en**	arbeit-**en**	fahr-**en**	nehm-**en**

The present tense forms of the auxiliary and modal verbs can be found in 7.1 and 7.2 (see p. 74ff.).

Verbs whose stem ends in **-t** or **-d** add an **-e-** before the endings **-st** or **-t** to make pronunciation easier:

reden *(to speak);* **arbeiten** *(to work):*

du red**e**st, er red**e**t;	*you speak, he speaks;*
ihr arbeit**e**t	*you work (plural)*

Infinitives, the 1st and 3rd person plural have the same form: **wohnen:** wir wohn**en**, sie/Sie wohn**en**.

Whether a verb is regular or irregular just has to be learnt by heart. In the appendix (p. 160ff.) you'll find a list of the most important irregular verbs.

8.2 Der Gebrauch des Präsens
The Use of the Present Tense
oder *Heute, morgen und überhaupt*

In German, the present tense can be used in so many various ways that we could almost regard it as a kind of universal tool. Its main function is to describe something happening in the present. But it can also convey a large number of other meanings:

something happening now	Anna **hält** eine Rede. *Anna is making a speech.*
something that happens regularly	Wir **treffen** uns montags um 10 Uhr zur Teambesprechung. *We meet every Monday at 10 for a team talk.*
a general rule	Die Sonne **geht** im Osten **auf**. *The sun rises in the east.*

something started in the past and is still going on	*Wir **sind** seit 10 Jahren verheiratet.* *We have been married for 10 years.*
something happening in the future	*Nächste Woche **kommt** die neue Personalchefin.* *The new head of personnel is coming next week.*
a story from the past told vividly	*Da waren wir also in Rom. Und wie ich so im Café **sitze**, da **kommt** Frau Smith von unserer Tochtergesellschaft in Los Angeles, und sie **sagt**: ...* *We were in Rome. And just as I'm sitting there in the café, in comes Frau Smith from our Los Angeles branch and she says to me: ...*

If the present tense is used to describe a future event, then an expression of time (adverb or adverbial phrase) should be used to make things clear: **nächste Woche, morgen, nächsten Montag** ... *(next week, tomorrow, next Monday ...).*

8.3 Der Imperativ
The Imperative
oder Befehle und Anweisungen geben

The imperative is used for orders, instructions, requests and advice made or given to another person directly. The imperative has the following forms:

	singular	plural
	address: *du*	address: *ihr*
informal **(no pronoun)**	**Nimm** doch Platz! *Take a seat.*	**Nehmt** doch Platz! *Take a seat.*
	Fahr vorsichtig! *Drive carefully.*	**Fahrt** vorsichtig! *Drive carefully.*
	Sei still! *Be quiet.*	**Seid** still! *Be quiet.*
formal **(pronoun** **obligatory)**	**Nehmen Sie** doch Platz! *Take a seat.*	**Nehmen Sie** doch Platz! *Take a seat.*
	Fahren Sie vorsichtig! *Drive carefully.*	**Fahren Sie** vorsichtig! *Drive carefully.*
	Seien Sie still! *Be quiet.*	**Seien Sie** still! *Be quiet.*

■ Informal imperative

The informal imperative singular is formed from the 2nd person singular of the present tense without **-st**; in the plural it is identical to the 2nd person plural:

du nimmst, imperative: ***nimm!*** *(take)*
ihr nehmt, imperative: ***nehmt!*** *(take)*

■ Formal imperative

Here the imperative is identical to the 3rd person plural present tense. The pronoun takes second place.

Sie nehmen, imperative: ***Nehmen Sie!*** *(take)*

In a sentence the imperative comes first (see 6, p. 67ff.). With separable verbs the inflected part comes first and the separable part at the end of the sentence. A sentence can, however, also start with **bitte** or the name of the person addressed.

order	Felix, **sitz**!	*Felix, sit!*
instruction	**Schneiden Sie** das Gemüse in dünne Scheiben.	*Cut the vegetables into thin slices.*
request	Frau Schweizer, **bringen Sie** mir bitte das Angebot der Firma Etech.	*Frau Schweitzer, bring me that offer from Etech would you, please.*
	Bitte **melden Sie** uns zu dieser Konferenz **an**!	*Please let them know we wish to attend the conference.*
advice	**Probier** doch mal die Atemübungen zur Stressbewältigung **aus**.	*Try breathing exercises to relieve stress.*

A "bare" imperative is very direct and can often sound curt, if not a little rude. It becomes much more polite through the use of **bitte** *(please)*, suitable modal particles and, of course, friendly intonation or even smiling.

Verbinden Sie mich **bitte** mit Herrn Gässlein!	*Please put me through to Herr Gässlein!*
Halt **doch bitte** hier **mal** an!	*Stop here, please, will you.*

EXERCISE 14 — Please put the following sentences into the imperative using the word *bitte*.

1. Sie sollten sich um den Job als Trainee bewerben.
2. Du solltest an dem Kurs in der Sprachenschule teilnehmen.
3. Sie sollten nicht im Gang rauchen.
4. Du solltest fragen, wenn dir eine Redewendung nicht bekannt ist.
5. Ihr solltet pünktlich kommen.

9 Präteritum, Perfekt und Plusquamperfekt
Past Simple, Present Perfect and Past Perfect

oder

Über die Vergangenheit sprechen
Talking about the Past

> Und, wie hat dir der Film gefallen?
>
> Echt super, war total spannend. Und die Schauspieler waren wirklich gut, obwohl es ja lauter unbekannte Leute waren. Hast du eigentlich das Buch schon gelesen?
>
> Ich wollte es eigentlich im Urlaub lesen ...

Peter: Well, how did you like the film? – Alan: Super film, it was really exciting. And the actors were excellent, even though none of them were famous. Have you read the book? – Peter: I was going to read it while I'm on holiday ...

Before you start thinking you're in the wrong film with all this talk about the past, here's a short explanation of the relevant past tense forms in German. But be careful: some of the terms used correspond with their English equivalent and some don't.

To talk about the past in German we almost always use the **Perfekt** or perfect tense. Sometimes this is used in exactly the same way as in English (i.e. the present perfect) but more often than not it is used in the same way as the English simple past. This is an important contrast that you need to remember.

Peter: Und, wie **hat** dir der Film **gefallen?**	*Peter: Well, how did you like the film?*

When using auxiliary and modal verbs and in more formal situations, however, the **Präteritum** or past simple is preferred. This is also true in written language.

Alan: Echt super, **war** total spannend.	*Super film, it was really exciting.*
Peter: Ich **wollte** es eigentlich im Urlaub **lesen ...**	*I was going to read it while I'm on holiday.*
Zeitungsmeldung:	newspaper article:
Auf der eisglatten Straße kam das Fahrzeug ins Schleudern und geriet auf die andere Fahrbahn.	*On the icy road the car skidded and swerved into oncoming traffic.*

To complete the spectrum of past tense forms the third tense we need to talk about is the **Plusquamperfekt** or past perfect tense.

That was the trailer – now we can start the main feature film with more detailed information.

9.1 Das Präteritum
The Past Simple
oder *Es war einmal*

The **Präteritum** or past simple in German is formed differently depending on whether the verb is regular and weak or irregular and strong.

■ Irregular verbs *(Starke Verben)*

These verbs change the vowel in their main stem. They have normal personal endings:

geben	Präteritum/past simple:	*Früher **gab** es viele Dinosaurier.* *In earlier times there were lots of dinosaurs.*
gehen	Präteritum/past simple:	*Wir **gingen** ins Kino.* *We went to the cinema.* stem + ending

■ Regular verbs *(Schwache Verben)*

Regular verbs do not change the vowel in their main stem. The past simple tense is indicated instead by the addition of **-(e)te-** after the main stem:

leben	Präteritum/past simple:	*Die Dinosaurier **lebte**n vor Millionen von Jahren.* *The dinosaurs lived millions of years ago.* stem + **-te-** + ending

In the past simple tense (**Präteritum**) both weak and strong verbs take the normal endings in all persons, which means no endings in the 1st and 3rd person singular and endings in the plural and in the 2nd person singular (see 7, p. 73).

The following table will help you to remember.

	leben *(weak)*	antworten *(weak)*	geben *(strong)*	rufen *(strong)*
ich	leb-**te**	antwort-**ete**	gab	rief
du	leb-**te-st**	antwort-**ete-st**	gab-**st**	rief-**st**
er/es/sie	leb-**te**	antwort-**ete**	gab	rief
wir	leb-**te-n**	antwort-**ete-n**	gab-**en**	rief-**en**
ihr	leb-**te-t**	antwort-**ete-t**	gab-**t**	rief-**t**
sie/Sie	leb-**te-n**	antwort-**ete-n**	gab-**en**	rief-**en**

 Verbs whose stem ends in **-d, -t, -m** or **-n**, indicate the Präteritum/past simple tense by adding **-ete-**.

■ **Mixed verbs** *(Mischverben)*

Some verbs change their main vowel like a strong verb but still take the weak verb ending *-(e)te-* for the Präteritum:

brennen Präteritum/past simple: *Die Lagerhallen bra**nn**ten.*
The warehouses were burning.
stem + *-te-* + ending

Here you can see that the past simple (**Präteritum**) in German can also express the continuous or progressive form that you know from English.

There's no easy way around it unfortunately: you just have to learn the strong and mixed verbs and their correct forms. There's a list on page 160ff. to help you.

■ **Modal verbs** *(Modalverben)*

Modal verbs form the **Präteritum**/past simple tense in the same way as weak verbs, but they lose their Umlaut in the process.

	dürfen	können	müssen	wollen	mögen	sollen
ich	durf-**te**	konn-**te**	muss-**te**	woll-**te**	moch-**te**	soll-**te**
du	durf-**te-st**	konn-**te-st**	muss-**te-st**	woll-**te-st**	mocht-**te-st**	soll-**te-st**
er/es/ sie	durf-**te**	konn-**te**	muss-**te**	woll-**te**	moch-**te**	soll-**te**
wir	durf-**te-n**	konn-**te-n**	muss-**te-n**	woll-**te-n**	moch-**te-n**	soll-**te-n**
ihr	durf-**te-t**	konn-**te-t**	muss-**te-t**	woll-**te-t**	moch-**te-t**	soll-**te-t**
sie/Sie	durf-**te-n**	konn-**te-n**	muss-**te-n**	woll-**te-n**	moch-**te-n**	soll-te-n

Auxiliary verbs have quite different forms in the past simple
(**Präteritum**):

	sein	haben	werden
ich	war	hat-**te**	wur-**de**
du	war-**st**	hat-**te-st**	wur-**de-st**
er/es/sie	war	hat-**te**	wur-**de**
wir	war-**en**	hat-**te-n**	wur-**de-n**
ihr	war-**t**	hat-**te-t**	wur-**de-t**
sie/Sie	war-**en**	hat-**te-n**	wur-**de-n**

9.2 Das Partizip II
The Past Participle
oder *Gelernt ist gelernt*

We need the past (or: perfect) participle (**Partizip II**) to form the present
perfect tense (**Perfekt**), but it is also used in the past perfect tense
(**Plusquamperfekt**).

■ **Present Perfect** *(Perfekt)*

> *Igor hat Elena eine E-Mail* **geschrieben**. (← schreiben)
> *Igor has written/wrote Elena an Email.*
>
> *Elena hat zuerst nicht* **gewusst**, *ob sie zurückschreiben soll.* (← wissen)
> *Elena didn't know at first whether she should reply.*
>
> *Aber dann hat Elena doch* **geantwortet**. (← antworten)
> *But then Elena did answer after all.*

■ **Past Perfect** *(Plusquamperfekt)*

> *Weil er die Unterlagen* **vergessen** *hatte, musste er zurück ins Büro.*
> *Because he had forgotten the papers, he had to go back to the office.*

There are numerous ways to form the past participle. Here is a short summary followed by a more detailed explanation.

infinitive	past participle				
	prefix	ge-	stem	ending	
studieren	–	–	studier-	-t	*study*
kaufen	–	ge-	-kauf-	-t	*buy*
einkaufen	ein-	-ge-	-kauf-	-t	*do some shopping*
verkaufen	ver-	–	-kauf-	-t	*sell*
sprechen	–	ge-	-sproch-	-en	*speak*
ansprechen	an-	-ge-	-sproch-	-en	*speak to s.o.*
versprechen	ver-	–	-sproch-	-en	*promise*
denken	–	ge-	-dach-	-t	*think*

The easiest verbs to deal with are those ending in *-ieren:*

infinitive		past participle	
studieren	→	studiert	*study*
demonstrieren	→	demonstriert	*demonstrate*
fotokopieren	→	fotokopiert	*photocopy*

To form the past participle we simply replace the infinitive ending *-en* with *-t*. It may encourage you to know that the number of verbs in this group is constantly increasing due to the adoption into German of new international words from other languages.

With all other verbs the matter is somewhat more complicated. Try to imagine verbs as the population of a country. There you have average citizens – these are our weak or regular verbs (***schwache/regelmäßige Verben***) and they form the largest section of the population. The past participle of these verbs has two identification marks: the prefix ***ge-*** and the participle ending *-(e)t* which replaces the infinitive ending *-en*. The main part of the verb remains unchanged.

infinitive	past participle	
kaufen →	gekauft	*buy – bought*
arbeiten →	gearbeitet	*work – worked*
spielen →	gespielt	*play – played*

Of course, even average citizens are not all the same and weak verbs can be divided into:

■ Simple verbs

kaufen	**ge**kauft	**ge-** at the beginning	*buy – bought*

■ Verbs with separable prefix

einkaufen	ein**ge**kauft	**ge-** between prefix and main stem	*buy – bought*

■ Verbs with inseparable prefix

verkaufen	verkauft	no **ge-**	*sell – sold*

Every country has its average citizens, but it also has people who don't conform. You might call them revolutionaries or rebels who in their various ways are just different. These would be our strong or irregular verbs (***starke/unregelmäßige Verben***).

They take on only the **ge-** as identification. The ending **-en** remains the same as in the infinitive. Many of them do, however, change the main stem.

infinitive	past participle	
sprechen →	**ge**sprochen	*speak – spoken*
kommen →	**ge**kommen	*come – come*
nehmen →	**ge**nommen	*take – taken*

Our rebels, too, can be divided into:

■ Simple verbs

sprechen → **ge**sprochen	**ge-** at the beginning *speak – spoken*

■ Verbs with separable prefix

ansprechen → an**ge**sprochen	**ge-** between prefix and main stem	*speak to – spoken to*

■ Verbs with inseparable prefix

versprechen → versprochen	no **ge-**	*promise – promised*

Rebel groups often cause problems. It's no different with German verbs.

Next we have a group we might call the "spies" or "undercover agents". They are the smallest group of all and they look a bit like ordinary citizens but with a few rebel elements thrown in. These are the so-called mixed verbs (**gemischte Verben**). They change their stem, but have both **ge-** and the ending **-(e)t** in the past participle (**Partizip II**) nevertheless.

infinitive	past participle	
denken	**ge**dach**t**	*think – thought*
bringen	**ge**brach**t**	*bring – brought*
rennen	**ge**rann**t**	*run – run*

Once again there's no way round it: you just have to learn the irregular and mixed verbs. It's easiest if you learn them in groups according to the way they change their main vowel. There are three possibilities:

A – B – A:	schlafen	– schlief	– geschlafen
A – B – B:	fliegen	– flog	– geflogen
A – B – C:	sprechen	– sprach	– gesprochen

In the appendix you'll find a list of the most important irregular and mixed verbs. To finish off this section here is a short survey:

verb type	infinitive	past participle	prefix	ge-	stem can change	ending
-ieren	studieren	studiert	no	no	no	**-(e)t**
simple	kaufen	gekauft	no	yes	no	**-(e)t**
verbs	sprechen	gesprochen	no	yes	yes	**-(e)n**
	denken	gedacht	no	yes	yes	**-(e)t**
verbs with	einkaufen	eingekauft	yes	yes	no	**-(e)t**
separable	an-	ange-				
prefix	sprechen	sprochen	yes	yes	yes	**-(e)n**
verbs with	verkaufen	verkauft	yes	no	no	**-(e)t**
inseparable	ver-	ver-				
prefix	sprechen	sprochen	yes	no	yes	**-(e)n**

As you can see, verbs ending in **-ieren** have neither prefix nor **ge-**. The stem remains the same and the ending is **-(e)t**. With simple verbs, verbs with separable and with inseparable prefix the verb stem may remain the same or it may change – there are various possibilities. Whether the verb stem changes or not doesn't depend on the prefix or whether **ge-** is used. Normally the ending **-(e)t** is used if the verb stem remains the same, and the ending **-(e)n** if the verb stem changes. Several irregular verbs change the stem only in the past simple – it stays the same in the past participle. The ending, however, is **-(e)n** nevertheless. And last of all, mixed verbs: they change their stem but have the ending **-(e)t**.

9.3 Das Perfekt
The Present Perfect
<u>oder</u> *Sein oder haben?*

Ja, ja, sein oder nicht sein ... wenn ich jetzt nicht schnellstens etwas esse, bin ich bald nicht mehr!

Genau, das war Hamlet, jetzt kommt das Kotelett!

Alan: Yes, yes, to be or not to be ... if I don't get something to eat soon, I will cease to be! – Peter: Exactly, but that was Hamlet, now comes the cutlet!

The question of whether to use **sein** or **haben** to form the present perfect tense (**Perfekt**) is a key issue. It is formed using the present tense of either **sein** or **haben** together with the past participle.

Wir **sind** gestern ins Kino **gegangen** und **haben** einen schönen Film **gesehen**.	*We went to the cinema yesterday and saw a great film.*

But when do we use **sein** and when do we use **haben**?

■ The Present Perfect with **sein**

Sein is used to form the present perfect in only very few cases. It's easiest and best, therefore, if you just learn this small group and then use **haben** for all the rest.

We use **sein** in the present perfect of the following verbs:

sein	**ist** gewesen	*be – has been/was*
bleiben	**ist** geblieben	*stay – has stayed/stayed*
werden	**ist** geworden	*become – has become/became*

passieren, geschehen and verbs with similar meaning:

| **passieren** | **ist** passiert | *happen – has happened/happened* |
| **geschehen** | **ist** geschehen | *happen – has happened/happened* |

Verbs indicating movement from A to B:

| Herr Schneider **ist** zur Messe nach Leipzig **gefahren**. | *Herr Schneider has gone to the fair in Leipzig.* |
| Maria **ist** kurz in den Keller **gegangen**. | *Maria has just gone down to the cellar.* |

Verbs indicating a change of state:

| Jan **ist** während des Vortrags von Herrn Verhusen **eingeschlafen**. | *Jan fell asleep during Herr Verhusen's talk.* |
| Kind, du **bist** aber **gewachsen**! | *How you've grown, child!* |

■ The Present Perfect with **haben**

Most verbs form the present perfect tense with **haben,** especially reflexive verbs, verbs that take an accusative object and modal verbs.

Reflexive verbs:
*Herr Niemer **hat sich** gut auf die Besprechung **vorbereitet**.*

Herr Niemer has prepared well for the meeting.

Verbs with an accusative object:
*Nina **hat** ihr Motorrad in die Garage **gefahren**.*

Nina has driven her motorbike into the garage.

Modal verbs:
*Das tut mir Leid, ich **habe** das nicht **gewollt**.*

I'm sorry, I didn't want that to happen.

Modal verbs are very often used in the present perfect. Normally they are used in the past simple (**Präteritum**).

Verbs that, due to the addition of a prefix, take on a different meaning may need either **sein** or **haben**.

Er hat gestanden.
Er ist aufgestanden.

He has admitted it.
He has got up.

9.4 Das Plusquamperfekt
The Past Perfect
<u>oder</u> *Ich hatte schon vergessen...*

The past perfect (**Plusquamperfekt**) indicates a time before the "normal" past. It is used to describe an event that happened before another event in the past.

*Als wir in Paris ankamen, **hatten** unsere Geschäftspartner bereits alles für die Konferenz **vorbereitet**.*
When we arrived in Paris, our business partners had already prepared everything for the conference.

> *Bevor wir weggefahren sind, **hatte** ich alle Pflanzen **gegossen**.*
> *Before we left, I had watered all the plants.*

Nachdem Frau Malina die neuen Teammitglieder **begrüßt hatte**, arbeiteten wir konsequent die Tagesordnung durch.	*After Frau Malina had greeted the new team members, we went through the agenda thoroughly.*

Forming the past perfect (**Plusquamperfekt**) is very easy. It's done in exactly the same way as the present perfect (**Perfekt)**, but instead of using the present tense (**Präsens**) of **sein** or **haben**, we use the past simple (**Präteritum**).

present perfect	past perfect
Wir **haben** die Verträge abgeschlossen. *We have concluded the contracts.*	Wir **hatten** die Verträge abgeschlossen. *We had concluded the contracts.*
Ihr **seid** zur Besprechung gekommen. *You have come to the meeting.*	Ihr **wart** zur Besprechung gekommen. *You had come to the meeting.*

Here is a short survey of the forms of the past perfect:

ich	hatte	gesagt	war	gekommen
du	hattest	gesagt	warst	gekommen
er/es/sie	hatte	gesagt	war	gekommen
wir	hatten	gesagt	waren	gekommen
ihr	hattet	gesagt	wart	gekommen
sie/Sie	hatten	gesagt	waren	gekommen

EXERCISE 15a Please put the following sentences into the Präteritum (simple past) and Perfekt (present perfect)

1. Herr White bucht für Donnerstag einen Flug nach Deutschland.
2. Er kommt am Flughafen Berlin-Tegel an und steigt in das nächste Taxi.
3. Dieses fährt Herrn White in das Hotel „Zum Goldenen Stern".
4. An der Rezeption erhält er die Schlüssel für sein Zimmer.
5. Um 15.00 Uhr trifft sich Herr White mit seinen Geschäftspartnern.
6. Diese erklären ihm die neue geschäftliche Situation und bitten um Verständnis.
7. Herr White unterbricht die Verhandlungen und zieht einen neuen Termin in Betracht.
8. Am nächsten Morgen holt Herr White seine Frau vom Flughafen ab.
9. Gemeinsam verbringen sie einige Tage in Berlin.
10. Frau und Herr White sehen sich noch am selben Tag das Brandenburger Tor an.
11. Am folgenden Tag besichtigen sie den Reichstag.
12. Am letzten Tag ihres Urlaubs fahren sie auf den Fernsehturm und werfen einen Blick auf die Dächer Berlins.

EXERCISE 15b Please put those parts of the following sentences in bold print into the Plusquamperfekt (past perfect).

1. **Nachdem wir einen Nachsendeauftrag bei der Post stellten,** fuhren wir in den Urlaub.
2. **Nachdem Eileen die Führerscheinprüfung bestand,** feierten wir das erfreuliche Ereignis mit einem Gläschen Sekt.
3. **Nachdem Marcus die Vor- und Nachteile darstellte,** gingen wir zur Aussprache über.
4. **Nachdem der Chef von seinem Auslandsreise zurückkam,** wurde das umstrittene Projekt nochmals besprochen.
5. **Nachdem die Abteilungsleiter eintrafen,** diskutierten wir über das weitere Vorgehen.

10 Das Futur
The Future Tense

oder

Über die Zukunft sprechen
Talking about the Future

Was werden Sie nach dem Praktikum machen?

Wenn ich das Praktikum abgeschlossen haben werde, werde ich nach Hause zurückfahren und mein Studium beenden – da liegt noch eine schwierige Prüfung vor mir.

Sie werden das schon schaffen!

*Colleague: What will you do after your work-experience programme? –
Alan: When I've finished the programme, I'm going to go back home and
finish my studies – I've still got a difficult exam to face. –
Colleague: You'll manage it!*

Although you can quite easily use the present tense (**Präsens**) in German to talk about the future (see 8, p. 85ff.), there are also special future tense forms.

10.1 Das Futur I
The Future Tense
oder Sie werden es schaffen

We use the future tense (**Futur I**) to talk about an event in the future or to express what we expect or assume will take place.

- Event in the future

Wir **werden** (im Sommer) nach Gran Canaria **fliegen**.	*We are going to fly to Gran Canaria in the summer.*

- Expectation

Hans **wird** dir sicherlich ein Souvenir **mitbringen**.	*Hans will certainly bring you back a souvenir.*

- Assumption

Bei dem Schneetreiben **werden** sich die Gäste wahrscheinlich **verspäten**.	*In this snowstorm the guests will probably be late.*
Wir **werden** im Sommer vielleicht nach Gran Canaria **fliegen**.	*Perhaps we'll fly to Gran Canaria in the summer.*

The future tense is formed with the present tense of the verb **werden** plus the infinitive.

	werden	+	infinitive
ich	werde		feiern
du	wirst		feiern
er/es/sie	wird		feiern
wir	werden		feiern
ihr	werdet		feiern
sie/Sie	werden		feiern

In any one sentence you use **werden** only once:

Mach dir keine Sorgen.	*Don't worry.*
Das **wird** schon gut (werden).	*It'll be OK.*

10.2 Das Futur II
The Future Perfect Tense
oder *Sie werden es geschafft haben*

The future perfect tense (**Futur II**) is used far less frequently than the future tense (**Futur I**). But you ought to be able to recognise and understand it when it occurs. We use the future perfect tense to talk about an event that will be completed in the future.

In zwei Jahren **wirst** du dein Studium **abgeschlossen haben**.	*In two years you will have finished your studies.*
Nächsten Freitag um diese Uhrzeit **werden** wir die Präsentation bereits hinter uns **gebracht haben**.	*By this time next Friday we will have already done the presentation.*

We can also use the future perfect to express an assumption about a past event.

> Herr Miller **wird** uns **geschrieben haben**, als wir im Urlaub waren.
>
> *Herr Miller will haven written to us while we were on holiday.*

The future perfect tense is formed using the present tense of the verb **werden** plus the past participle plus **haben** or **sein.**

> Ende des Jahres **werden** wir **gefeiert haben** und viele Gäste **werden gekommen sein**.
>
> *At the end of the year we will have had our party and lots of guests will have come.*

> 2005 **werden** wir die Filiale **eröffnet haben** und die Presse **wird** dabei **gewesen sein**.
>
> *In 2005 our new branch we will have opened and the press will have been there.*

 We often use the present perfect (**Perfekt**) in German instead of the future perfect (**Futur II**).

> In zwei Jahren **hast** du dein Studium **abgeschlossen**.
>
> *In two years you will have finished your studies.*

> Nächsten Freitag um diese Uhrzeit **haben** wir die Präsentation bereits hinter uns **gebracht**.
>
> *By this time next Friday we will have already done the presentation.*

EXERCISE 16 Please put all the sentences in exercise 15 into the future tense.

---

11 Der Konjunktiv
The Subjunctive

oder

Wünsche und indirekte Rede
Wishes and Reported Speech

Alan: I heard today that one of my colleagues won 200,000 euros on
the lottery. – Peter: Wow, if that happened to me, I'd give up my job
straight away and I'd go on a long trip somewhere. And what will your
colleague do with it all? – Alan: I was told he wanted to found his own
firm and would use the money as starting capital.

It's nice to dream, isn't it? But there's no need for you to dream about mastering the subjunctive (**Konjunktiv**) any more. When you've done this chapter, your dream is bound to come true!

11.1 Der Konjunktiv I
The Present Subjunctive
oder Aussagen wiedergeben

The present subjunctive (**Konjunktiv I**) occurs nearly always in written language only and is used exclusively to express indirect or reported speech (**indirekte Rede**). Colloquially, indirect speech is usually expressed using the same forms of the verb as in direct speech (**direkte Rede**).

> Direct speech:
> Michael: „Ich **kann** am Samstag leider nicht zur Party **kommen**."
> *Michael: "I can't come to the party on Saturday unfortunately."*
>
> Reported speech (colloquial):
> Anke: „Michael sagte, dass er am Samstag nicht zur Party **kommen kann**."
> *Anke: "Michael said that he can't come to the party on Saturday."*
>
> Reported speech (formal) with present subjunctive:
> Anke: „Michael sagte, dass er am Samstag nicht zur Party **kommen könne**."
> *Anke: "Michael said that he couldn't come to the party on Saturday."*

The present subjunctive is formed as follows:
Main stem of the infinitive without an ending + **-e-** + normal ending for the appropriate person. (See 7, p. 73.) A double **-e** disappears.

present subjunctive	
ich	hab-e
du	hab-e-st
er/es/sie	hab-e
wir	hab-e-n
ihr	hab-e-t
sie/Sie	hab-e-n

The forms of the present subjunctive are sometimes identical to those of the present indicative. When this happens in reported speech, we fall back on the past subjunctive (**Konjunktiv II**) or **würde +** infinitive (see 11.2, p. 113).

Direct speech:
*Mona: „Die koreanischen Partner **bleiben** eine Woche."*
Mona: "Our Korean partners are staying for a week."

Reported speech with present subjunctive:
*Jan: „Mona sagt, die koreanischen Partner **bleiben** eine Woche."*
Jan: "Mona says our Korean partners are staying for a week."

Reported speech with past subjunctive:
*Jan: „Mona sagt, die koreanischen Partner **würden** eine Woche **bleiben**."*
Jan: "Mona says our Korean partners are staying for a week."

The verb **sein** (*to be*) is once again a special case.

present subjunctive	
ich	sei
du	seist
er/es/sie	sei
wir	seien
ihr	sei(e)t
sie/Sie	seien

The present subjunctive is most often used in the 3rd person singular:

> er/es/sie **habe**
> er/es/sie **werde**
> er/es/sie **müsse**
> er/es/sie **wolle**
> er/es/sie **könne**
> er/es/sie **kaufe**
> ...

What else do we need to know about reported speech? It is introduced by a main clause (**Hauptsatz**) containing a verb of "saying" or "reporting".

Der Pressesprecher **sagte**, dass es sich dabei nur um ein Gerücht **handle**.	*The press spokesman said that it's only a rumour.*
Martina **sagt**, Ulrike **sei** krank.	*Martina says Ulrike is ill.*

The personal pronouns may change.

direct speech	reported speech
Bozena: „**Ich** nehme ein Taxi." *Bozena: "I'll take a taxi."*	Martha: „Bozena sagt, **sie** nehme ein Taxi." *Martha: "Bozena says she'll take a taxi."*
Die Teammitglieder: „**Wir** brauchen mehr Zeit." *The team: "We need more time."*	Die Chefsekretärin: „Die Teammitglieder sagen, **sie** brauchen mehr Zeit." *The boss's secretary: "The team say they need more time."*

11.2 Der Konjunktiv II
The Past Subjunctive
oder *Hätte ich nur, dann würde ich jetzt...*

The past subjunctive (**Konjunktiv II**) serves either as a substitute for the present subjunctive (see 11.1, p. 111), or it is used to express an unreal condition, a presumption or speculation or a polite wish or request.

Substitute for the present subjunctive:
*Mira sagt, die Jungs **hätten** zu viel **getrunken**.*   *Mira says the boys drank too much.*

An unreal condition:
*Wenn ich reich **wäre**, **würde** ich den Winter immer im Süden **verbringen**.*   *If I were rich, I'd spend the winter down south.*

Presumption/speculation:
*Es **könnte** ja auch sein, dass Hans noch im Stau steht.*   *It could well be that Hans is still caught up in a traffic jam.*

Polite wish or request:
*Herr Bisowski, **könnten** Sie mit bitte die Unterlagen der Firma Fallmer bringen?*   *Herr Bisowski, could you bring me the Fallmer documents, please?*

The past subjunctive is formed in two different ways:

■ With weak verbs the past subjunctive and the past simple are identical:

past simple: ***ich reiste ...***
past subjunctive: ***ich reiste ...***

To avoid confusion a substitute form is used:
würde (= past subjunctive of **werden**) + infinitive

*ich **würde reisen***   *I travelled/I would travel*
*du **würdest kochen***   *you cooked/you would cook*

■ With strong verbs, on the other hand, the past simple forms the base:

The signal ending **-e** is added together with an **Umlaut** on the main vowel.

ich kä**me** (← kommen; past simple: ich kam)
I came/I would come

er trä**fe** (← treffen; past simple: er traf)
he met/he would meet

sie schrieb**e** (← schreiben; past simple: sie schrieb)
she wrote/she would write

Nevertheless, even with strong verbs, especially in everyday speech, we use **würde** + infinitive. It is the most common form of the past subjunctive in German.

	werden +	infinitive
ich	würde	fragen
du	würdest	fragen
er/es/sie	würde	fragen
wir	würden	fragen
ihr	würdet	fragen
sie/Sie	würden	fragen

It's only in the case of auxiliary and modal verbs that we find independent forms of the past subjunctive in common use.

infinitive	sein	haben	dürfen	können	müssen	wollen	sollen
past simple	er war	er hatte	er durfte	er konnte	er musste	er wollte	er sollte
past subjunctive							
ich	wär-*e*	hätt-*e*	dürft-*e*	könnt-*e*	müsst-*e*	wollt-*e*	sollt-*e*
du	wär-*(e)st*	hätt-*est*	dürft-*est*	könnt-*est*	müsst-*est*	wollt-*est*	sollt-*est*
er/es/ sie	wär-*e*	hätt-*e*	dürft-*e*	könnt-*e*	müsst-*e*	wollt-*e*	sollt-*e*
wir	wär-*en*	hätt-*en*	dürft-*en*	könnt-*en*	müsst-*en*	wollt-*en*	sollt-*en*
ihr	wär-*(e)t*	hätt-*et*	dürft-*et*	könnt-*et*	müsst-*et*	wollt-*et*	sollt-*et*
sie/Sie	wär-*en*	hätt-*en*	dürft-*en*	könnt-*en*	müsst-*en*	wollt-*en*	sollt-*en*

The past perfect subjunctive is formed using the past subjunctive of **sein** or **haben** + the past participle (**Partizip II**).

Wir **wären** ja gerne zum Frühlingsfest **gekommen,** aber wir waren leider verhindert.

We would have liked to come to the spring party, but something came up unfortunately.

Wenn die Besprechung gestern Abend nicht so lange **gedauert hätte, wäre** ich sicher noch ins Training **gekommen**.

If the meeting yesterday evening hadn't lasted so long, I would have made it to training for sure.

E X E R C I S E   1 7 a **Please change the direct speech in the following sentences into reported speech.**

1. Herr Miller sagt: „Ich bin mit meiner neuen Marketingassistentin sehr zufrieden."
2. Frau Dinz erläutert: „Durch das neue Computerprogramm können wir die Absatzzahlen schneller ermitteln."
3. Der Verkäufer erklärt: „Das neue Handy verfügt über eine USB-Schnittstelle."
4. Die Angestellte erwidert: „Durch mehr Personal erreichen wir eine bessere Kundenbindung."
5. Der Chef sagt: „Ich bin mit der Arbeitsweise von Frau Gordon sehr zufrieden."
6. Leyla fragt ihre Kollegin: „Für welchen Zeitraum hast du deinen Urlaub eingeplant?"

E X E R C I S E   1 7 b **Please complete the following sentences with the correct form of the verb in the past subjunctive.**

1. _____ ich Sie kurz stören? (dürfen)

2. _____ du das für mich kopieren? (können)

3. Das _____ wirklich nett von dir. (sein)

4. Ich habe keine eigene Firma. Aber wenn ich eine eigene Firma

    _____, dann _____ ich mit den Mitarbeitern jeden Morgen

    Tai-Chi _____. (haben/machen)

5. So eine Katastrophe! Das alles _____ nicht _____,

    wenn ich besser _____ _____ (passieren/aufpassen)!

---

12 Das Passiv
The Passive

oder

Wer etwas macht, ist nicht wichtig
The person or "doer" is not important

Also ... die Regalfüße sind schon in der Boden-platte verschraubt, sehr praktisch, dann werden jetzt erst mal diese Seitenteile an der Bodenplatte festgemacht ... so – und dann ...

... dann muss noch das Stützkreuz hingeschraubt werden ... Wo ist es denn nur?

Peter: Right then ... the feet are already screwed into the base, that's handy, now these side pieces get fixed to the base ... like this – and then ... – Alan: ... then the cross support has to be screwed in ... Where is it by the way?

In the passive form of the verb it's not the person that's important but what happens. The passive is used to express what happens to a thing or person, not what a thing or person does. The actual doer is not important, not identifiable or needs to remain unknown.

Das Regal **wird zusammen-gebaut**.	*The shelves are being put together.*
Die Seitenteile **werden** an der Bodenplatte **festgemacht**.	*The side pieces get fixed to the base.*
Der Auftrag **ist vergeben worden**.	*The job has been assigned.*

The passive tends to get used most in academic texts, lists of instructions etc. There are two forms: the passive describing an action and the passive describing a state.

12.1 Das Vorgangspassiv
The Passive Expressing Action
oder *Das Regal wird aufgebaut*

As in English, verbs with an accusative object almost always have a passive form. The accusative object in the active sentence becomes the subject of the passive sentence. If we still need to name the person involved, we add the preposition **von.**

active:	*Dr. Kappler untersucht **den Jungen**.*
	subject accusative object
	Dr. Kappler is examining the boy.
passive:	***Der Junge** wird (von Dr. Kappler) untersucht.*
	subject + auxiliary verb + (**von** + agent) past participle
	werden
	The boy is being examined (by Dr. Kappler).

Sometimes **von** is replaced by **durch.**

Die Häuser **wurden** (durch das Erdbeben) schwer **beschädigt**.
subject + auxiliary verb + (**durch** + agent) past participle
werden
The houses were badly damaged (by the earthquake).

Just like the active, the passive occurs in all tenses and also in the subjunctive. Formation follows the same system as the active, always using a form of the verb **werden**.

Here is a list of all the passive forms in the various tenses. It's a bit of a marathon, but you already know at least half of what follows, so there's no need to worry. Take courage in both hands and a deep breath!

■ Present Tense *(Präsens)*

	present tense of **werden**	+ past participle	
ich	werde	geliebt	*(Someone) loves me.*
du	wirst	angerufen	*There's a telephone call for you.*
er/es/sie	wird	gefüttert	*He/It/She is being fed.*
wir	werden	benachrichtigt	*We're getting the news.*
ihr	werdet	überrascht	*You'll be surprised.*
sie/Sie	werden	abgeholt	*They/You are getting picked up.*

As you can see from the English translation of the example sentences, the passive is often used in German to express a certain idea, whereas it would not be natural to use the passive in other languages. The opposite, of course, is also the case (see 12.2, p. 124 „man")! This is especially true for present tense forms. It is best, of course, to learn these in context since the choice of an active or passive construction always depends on the meaning of the individual verb and the intention of the speaker.

■ **Past Simple** *(Präteritum)*

	past simple of *werden* +	past participle	
ich	wurde	geliebt	*(Someone) loved me.*
du	wurdest	angerufen	*You got a telephone call.*
er/es/sie	wurde	gefüttert	*He/It/She was fed.*
wir	wurden	benachrichtigt	*We were informed.*
ihr	wurdet	überrascht	*You were surprised.*
sie/Sie	wurden	abgeholt	*They/You were picked up.*

■ **Present Perfect** *(Perfekt)*

The formation follows the same pattern as for all the other tenses: present perfect of **werden** *(e.g. ich bin geworden)* + past participle. There is just one small difference: in the passive we use **worden** instead of the normal past participle **geworden**.

	present tense of + *sein*	past participle +	*worden*	
ich	bin	geliebt	worden	*(Someone) loved me.*
du	bist	angerufen	worden	*You got a telephone call.*
er/es/sie	ist	gefüttert	worden	*He/It/She has been fed.*
wir	sind	benachrichtigt	worden	*We have been informed.*
ihr	seid	überrascht	worden	*You have been surprised.*
sie/Sie	sind	abgeholt	worden	*They/You have been picked up.*

■ Past Perfect *(Plusquamperfekt)*

	past simple + of *sein*	past participle +	*worden*	
ich	war	geliebt	worden	*(Someone) had loved me.*
du	warst	angerufen	worden	*You had got a telephone call.*
er/es/sie	war	gefüttert	worden	*He/It/She had been fed.*
wir	waren	benachrichtigt	worden	*We had been informed.*
ihr	wart	überrascht	worden	*You had been surprised.*
sie/Sie	waren	abgeholt	worden	*They/You had been picked up.*

■ Future *(Futur I)*

	present tense of + *werden*	past participle +	*werden*	
ich	werde	geliebt	werden	*(Someone) will love me.*
du	wirst	angerufen	werden	*You will get a telephone call.*
er/es/sie	wird	gefüttert	werden	*He/It/She will be fed.*
...				

■ Future Perfect (Futur II)

	present tense of + werden	past participle +	worden sein	
ich	werde	geliebt	worden sein	*(Someone) will have loved me.*
du	wirst	angerufen	worden sein	*You will have got a telephone call.*
er/es/sie	wird	gefüttert	worden sein	*He/It/She will have been fed.*
...				

■ Present Subjunctive (Konjunktiv I Präsens)

	present subjunctive of werden	+ past participle	
ich	werde	geliebt	*(that) (someone) loves me.*
er/es/sie	werde	gefüttert	*(that) he/it/she is being fed.*

■ Past Subjunctive (Konjunktiv II Präsens)

	past subjunctive of werden	+ past participle	
ich	würde	geliebt	*(that) (someone) loved me.*
du	würdest	angerufen	*(that) you got a telephone call.*
er/es/sie	würde	gefüttert	*(that) he/it/she was being fed.*
...			

■ Past Perfect Subjunctive *(Konjunktiv II Perfekt)*

	past perfect subjunctive + of *sein*	past participle + *worden*		
ich	wäre	geliebt	worden	*(that) (someone) had/ would have loved me.*
du	wärest	angerufen	worden	*(that) you had/would have got a telephone call.*
er/es/sie	wäre	gefüttert	worden	*(that) he/it/she had/ would have been fed.*
...				

■ Passive of Modal Verbs

Do auxiliary verbs also have a passive form in German? Yes, of course they do – and when they occur there are all kinds of possibilities of forming a sentence.

The passive of modal verbs is formed like this:
modal verb form + past participle + **werden** in the infinitive

Marianne **soll** befördert **werden**.
(present)
Marianne is to be promoted.

Marianne **sollte befördert werden**.
(past simple)
Marianne was supposed to/should be promoted.

Marianne **hat befördert werden sollen**.
(present perfect)
Marianne was supposed to be promoted.

Marianne **hatte befördert werden sollen**.
(past perfect)
Marianne had been supposed to be promoted.

Marianne **hätte befördert werden sollen.**
(past subjunctive)
Marianne should have been promoted.

The present, past simple and past subjunctive are the forms normally in common use. The present perfect and past perfect occur only very rarely.

12.2 Passiv-Alternativen
Alternatives for the Passive
oder *Man baut das Regal so auf*

If you want to remain impersonal but don't want to use the passive, then there are several alternatives you can use in German. Some of them are similar in English, others completely different.

(1) *man*
(2) *sich lassen* + infinitive
(3) *ist, hat, gibt, bleibt, geht + zu* + infinitive
(4) adjectives derived from verbs ending in *-bar, -lich* or *-ig*

	passive	passive-alternative
(1)	Was kann da gemacht werden? *What can be done?*	Was kann **man** da machen? *What can one do?*
(2)	Das kann eingerichtet werden. *That can be arranged.*	Das **lässt sich** schon **einrichten**. *That can be arranged.*
(3)	Es muss noch viel getan werden. *A lot still has to be done.*	Es **bleibt** noch viel **zu tun**. *A lot still remains to be done.*
(3)	Diese Akte muss kopiert werden. *This file must be copied.*	Diese Akte **ist zu kopieren**. *This file is to be copied.*

(4) *Dieses Vorgehen kann nicht*   *Dieses Vorgehen ist nicht*
    vertreten werden.   *vertret**bar**.*
    This procedure can't be justified. *This procedure is not justifiable.*

(4) *Der Patient kann nicht*   *Der Patient ist nicht transport-*
    transportiert werden.   *fäh**ig**.*
    The patient can't be moved.   *The patient is not capable of being
                                        moved.*

12.3 Das Zustandspassiv
The Passive Describing a State
<u>oder</u> *Das Regal ist aufgebaut*

*Eva: Ah, here you are. I thought you wanted to put those shelves up? –
Alan: The shelves are already up! – Eva: What? That was quick!*

There are two passive forms in German. Besides the passive describing actions or events, there is also the passive describing a state, a situation or a result (**Zustandspassiv**). The latter is not used as frequently.

Wir haben eine Stunde gearbeitet und jetzt **ist** das Regal **aufgebaut**.	*We worked for an hour and now the shelves are up.*
Mein Schreibtisch **ist aufgeräumt**.	*My desk is tidy.*
Die Haustür **ist** bereits **abgeschlossen**.	*The front door is already locked.*

Luckily, the passive describing a state occurs almost only in the present and past simple tenses. It is formed in a similar way to the passive describing events. There is only one difference: instead of a form of **werden**, the appropriate form of **sein** is used.

(1) **present tense:** present tense of **sein** + past participle
(2) **past simple:** past simple of **sein** + past participle

(1) Manchmal wünsche ich mir, ich komme ins Büro, der Kaffee **ist** schon **gekocht**, alle meine Arbeit **ist** bereits **getan** und meine Chefin **ist verreist**.
Sometimes I wish that when I get in to the office, the coffee has been made, all my work has already been done and my boss is away.

(2) Ich träumte kürzlich, ich kam von der Arbeit nach Hause und das Geschirr **war abgespült**, alles **war aufgeräumt**, die Wäsche **war gewaschen** und **gebügelt** und das Essen **war gekocht** und stand auf dem Tisch.
I dreamt recently that I came home from work and the washing-up had been done, everything had been tidied away, the washing and ironing had been finished and supper had been cooked and was on the table.

EXERCISE 18	Please form sentences using the passive in the past simple.

Example:

2002	Einführung des Euros als Bargeld und gesetzliches Zahlungsmittel

2002 wurde der Euro als Bargeld und gesetzliches Zahlungsmittel eingeführt.

1.	2000	Wahl von Wladimir Putin zum russischen Staatspräsidenten
2.	1999	Erweiterung der NATO
3.	1999	Wahl von Johannes Rau zum deutschen Bundespräsidenten
4.	1998	Eröffnung der Europäischen Zentralbank
5.	1998	Aufbau der ersten internationalen Raumstation ISS
6.	1993	Einrichtung der Europäischen Union
7.	1991	Start des Hubble-Teleskops
8.	1990	Wiedervereinigung der beiden deutschen Staaten

13 Die Präpositionen
Prepositions

oder

Auf, über, für & Co.
On, over, for & Co.

Trainer: And now with one leg at a time on to the step board – yes – with your arms held forward – over the step board to the other side – and let's do it with a smile ... – Alan: For over an hour now without a break ... – Peter: If you want to look good, then you've got to suffer ...

So you can keep in trim with your German, here is a short fitness course in prepositions (**Präpositionen**). Prepositions come before nouns or groups of nouns and dictate or determine what case the noun needs to be in: accusative, dative or genitive.

Some prepositions combine with the definite article to form one single word (see 1.2, p. 18f.), e.g. **zum** = **zu dem.**

13.1 Die Präpositionen mit Akkusativ
Prepositions with the Accusative
<u>oder</u> Durch, für, gegen & Co.

Some prepositions always take the accusative:

bis	**Bis nächsten Mittwoch** erwarte ich ein Ergebnis. *I expect a result by next Wednesday.*
	Er ist noch **bis einen Tag** nach Weihnachten in den USA. *He'll be in America till one day after Christmas.*
durch	Wir fahren gleich **durch einen langen Tunnel**. *In a minute we'll be driving through a long tunnel.*
	Unsere Firma geht zurzeit **durch eine schwierige Phase**. *Our firm is going through a difficult phase at the moment.*
für	Diese Rosen sind **für dich**. *These roses are for you.*
	Der Student bleibt **für drei Monate**. *The student is staying for three months.*
gegen	Frau Mino hat dieses Projekt **gegen den Willen** ihres Vorgesetzten durchgesetzt. *Frau Mino pushed this project through against her boss's will.*
	David ist mit dem Schlitten **gegen einen Baum** gefahren. *David crashed against a tree with his sledge.*

ohne	Herr Reyher hat die Rede **ohne seine Unterlagen** gehalten. *Herr Reyher made the speech without his notes.*
	Ich bin **ohne einen Cent** aus dem Haus gegangen. *I went out of the house without a cent.*
um	Nun rede doch nicht so **um den heißen Brei** herum. *Stop beating about the bush.*
	Um die Ecke ist ein Geldautomat. *There's a cash machine around the corner.*

Two other prepositions **entlang** and **betreffend** come after the noun. They don't occur very frequently.

Wir gehen den Strand **entlang** bis zum Hafen.	*We'll go along the beach as far as the harbour.*
Den Vertrag **betreffend** wollten wir noch anmerken …	*With refererence to the contract we just wanted to point out ….*

 The preposition **bis** is often used in combination with other prepositions which then determine the case.

Bis zum (dative) nächsten Mittwoch erwarte ich ein Ergebnis. *By next Wednesday I expect a result.*

13.2 Die Präpositionen mit Dativ
Prepositions with the Dative
oder Aus, bei, mit & Co.

The following prepositions always take the dative case:

ab	**Ab nächster Woche** gehe ich regelmäßig schwimmen. *From next week on I'm going swimming regularly.*

Ab dem ersten August ist Herr Radwan im Urlaub.
From the first of August Herr Radwan is on holiday.

aus   Wir müssen die Sitzung **aus wichtigen Gründen** verschieben.
We must postpone the meeting for important reasons.

Michael kommt gerade **aus dem Training**.
Michael is just coming back from training.

bei   Alan wohnt **bei seinem Freund**.
Alan is staying at his friend's house.

Bei mir gibt es so etwas nicht.
I don't have/wouldn't do anything like that.

gegenüber   **Gegenüber dem Firmengebäude** ist ein großer Park.
Opposite the office building is a large park.

Gegenüber der Bank ist ein Kiosk.
Opposite the bank is a kiosk.

mit   Raphael fährt **mit seinem Kollegen** zum Kongress.
Raphael is travelling with his colleague to the conference.

Wir machen unsere Arbeit **mit Engagement und Spaß**.
We do our work with commitment and pleasure.

nach   **Nach dem Mittagessen** muss ich zum Chef.
After lunch I have to go and see the boss.

Wir fahren am Wochenende **nach Paris**.
We're going to Paris at the weekend.

seit   Carmen wohnt **seit vielen Jahren** in Deutschland.
Carmen has been living in Germany for many years.

Seit einer Woche warte ich auf Ihren Rückruf!
I've been waiting for you to answer my call for a week!

von   Jonathan nimmt **vom ersten** bis zum zehnten Januar Urlaub.
Jonathan is having a holiday from the first till the tenth of January.

Unsere Kollegen kamen ganz begeistert **von der Messe** zurück.
Our colleagues came back from the fair full of enthusiasm.

zu   Ich gratuliere dir **zur Gehaltserhöhung**!
Congratulations on your salary increase.

Laura musste **zum Zahnarzt** gehen.
Laura had to go to the dentist.

13.3 Die Wechselpräpositionen
Prepositions that Vary
<u>oder</u> *Akkusativ oder Dativ?*

There are some prepositions that can take more than just one case. They are called **Wechselpräpositionen** (prepositions that can vary). They only ever indicate place or time:

an, auf, hinter, in, neben, über, unter, vor, zwischen.

an   Felix sitzt **an** der Wand.
Felix is sitting up against the wall.

auf   Der Ball liegt **auf** Felix' Nase.
The ball is on Felix's nose.

hinter   Der Ball liegt **hinter** Felix.
The ball is behind Felix.

in   Felix liegt **im** Korb.
Felix is lying in the basket.

neben *Der Ball liegt **neben** Felix.*
The ball is next to Felix.

 über *Felix springt **über** den Ball.*
Felix jumps/is jumping over the ball.

 unter *Der Ball liegt **unter** Felix.*
The ball is under(-neath) Felix.

 vor *Der Ball liegt **vor** Felix.*
The ball is in front of Felix.

 zwischen *Felix sitzt **zwischen** den Bällen.*
Felix is sitting between the balls.

It seems that these prepositions are not satisfied with exercising their influence in just one way. As a result they may choose the accusative or the dative case. There are rules, however, as to when and why.

Accusative is dyn$A$mic. It indicates movement: **wohin** *(where to)?* (ACTION)

Dative is static. It indicates place or movement within a limited place: **wo** *(where)?* (POSITION)

These examples will make things clear:

accusative: *Wohin?*	dative: *Wo?*
Wohin legst du die Akte? *Where are you putting the file?*	**Wo** ist denn die Akte? *Where is the file then?*
Ich lege/stelle die Akte ... *I'm putting it ...*	Die Akte liegt/steht ... *The file is ...*
an die Wand. *up against the wall.*	**an der** Wand. *up against the wall.* ▶

accusative: *Wohin?*	dative: *Wo?*
auf den Tisch. *on the table.*	**auf dem** Tisch. *on the table.*
hinter das Telefon. *behind the telephone.*	**hinter dem** Telefon. *behind the telephone.*
in den Ablagekorb. *in the filing-tray.*	**im** Ablagekorb. *in the filing-tray.*
neben den Ordner. *next to the ring-binder.*	**neben dem** Ordner. *next to the ring-binder.*
über die Bücher. *above the books.*	**über den** Büchern. *above the books.*
unter die Bücher. *under the books.*	**unter den** Büchern. *under the books.*
vor das Buch. *in front of the book.*	**vor dem** Buch. *in front of the book.*
zwischen die anderen Akten. *among the other files.*	**zwischen den** anderen Akten. *among the other files.*

13.4 Die Präpositionen mit Genitiv
Prepositions with the Genitive
oder *Wegen des Genitivs...*

There are quite a few prepositions that take the genitive. But nowadays they are used less and less. If they are used in colloquial speech, people tend to prefer using the dative instead. The most common prepositions taking the genitive are as follows:

aufgrund	**Aufgrund der schlechten Umsatzzahlen** im ersten Quartal wurde eine Krisensitzung einberufen. *Due to the poor turnover figures in the first quarter a crisis meeting was called.*

DIE PRÄPOSITIONEN

statt	*Ich hätte lieber Nudeln* **statt (der) Kartoffeln.**
	I'd rather have pasta instead of (the) potatoes.
trotz	**Trotz des schlechten Wetters** *fand das Fußballspiel statt.*
	colloquial often: **Trotz dem schlechten Wetter ...**
	In spite of the bad weather the football match took place.
während	**Während des Meetings** *ist Herr Maier fast eingeschlafen.*
	colloquial often: **Während dem Meeting ...**
	During the meeting Herr Maier almost fell asleep.
wegen	*Diana hat* **wegen des Streits** *mit ihrem Chef gekündigt.*
	colloquial often: ... **wegen dem Streit ...**
	Because of the dispute with her boss, Diana has resigned.

E X E R C I S E   1 9   **Please complete the following sentences using the correct case.**

1. *Die Abschlussfeier fand bei (mein Bruder Patrick) statt.*
2. *Der Autofahrer ist gegen (der Baum) gefahren.*
3. *Die Auszubildenden stehen im Kreis um (ihr Trainer).*
4. *Aufgrund (die Globalisierung) werden Sprachkenntnisse immer wichtiger.*
5. *Die Touristen-Information befindet sich gegenüber (das Rathaus).*
6. *Trotz (die zahlreichen Regeln) beherrscht Axel die deutsche Grammatik gut.*
7. *Seit (ein Jahr) hat Steve einen Job als Webdesigner.*
8. *Während (die Sommermonate) befinden sich im Bistro um die Ecke nur wenige Gäste.*
9. *Ramona ist am Wochenende zu (ihre Schwester) gefahren.*
10. *Der Bankangestellte holt das Geld aus (der Tresor).*
11. *Maggie und Geneviève haben für (der weltweite Friede) protestiert.*
12. *Der Schlüssel war zwischen (das Gepäck).*

14 Satzverbindungen
Sentence-Linkers

oder

Wie man Sätze verbindet
How to combine sentences

Alan: I need the allen key … and then you'll have to hold this part
steady … – Peter: I'll do anything to make sure my bike goes
again … – Alan: I'm sure that we'll be able to fix it, but first the wheel
has got to come off …

Although language bears little resemblance to a motorbike, certain parts
can be "bolted together" and taken apart again. It is possible to join
several sentences together – not with nuts and bolts, but with little
words called conjunctions (**Konjunktionen**). In German we divide these
conjunctions into two groups: coordinating conjunctions (**Konjunktionen**) and subordinating conjunctions (**Subjunktionen**).

14.1 Die Konjunktionen
Coordinating Conjunctions
oder Und, aber, denn & Co.

Coordinating conjunctions (**Konjunktionen**) can join two sentences or
main clauses together. The position of the verbs in both is the same.

conjunction	main focus of meaning	example
aber	limitation, contrast	*Bitte verlegen Sie den Termin mit Herrn Manger auf nächste Woche, **aber** seien Sie bitte sehr freundlich!* *Please postpone the appointment with Herr Manger till next week, but be nice about it.*
denn	reason	*Peter ist übers Wochenende zu seinen Eltern gefahren, **denn** sein Vater wird 70.* *Peter has gone to his parents for the weekend because it's his father's 70th birthday.*
doch	contrast	*Wir wollten am Sonntag zum Surfen gehen, **doch** es hat leider den ganzen Tag geregnet.* *We wanted to go surfing on Sunday, but unfortunately it rained all day.*

conjunction	main focus of meaning	example
oder	alternative	*Sollen wir zum Tauchen gehen* **oder** *wollen wir nur zum Baden fahren?* *Shall we go diving or just go for a swim?*
sondern	alternative	*Wir fliegen nicht nach Wien,* **sondern** *wir fahren mit dem Zug.* *We're not flying to Vienna but travelling by train.*
und	enumeration	*Alan ist jetzt schon zwei Monate in Deutschland* **und** *er fühlt sich sehr wohl hier.* *Alan has been in Germany now for two months and he feels very much at home here.*

14.2 Die Subjunktionen
Subordinating Conjunctions
<u>oder</u> *Dass, weil & Co.*

Subordinating conjunctions (**Subjunktionen**) connect a main clause with a subordinate clause. The subordinate clause can come before or after the main clause, but it can't stand on its own. Subordinate clauses have a different word order than main clauses (see 6, p. 67ff.). All the verbs come at the end of the clause.

Wir glauben, **dass** *Sie das gut* **verstehen können**.	*We believe that you can understand that.*
Ich frage mich, **ob** *Sie das schon* **verstanden haben**.	*I wonder whether you understood that.*

Now it's not exactly uncommon in German for several verbs to be used in one and the same sentence. When they occur in a subordinate clause, we have to ask ourselves how on earth they can all be arranged in some sort of order. You've probably already guessed that there are rules for this.

■ The conjugated verb comes right at the end:

Eva freut sich, weil sie eine neue Stelle bekommen **hat**.	*Eva is pleased because she's got a new job.*

■ A participle or an infinitive comes directly before the conjugated verb:

Ich komme, sobald ich diesen Text fertig geschrieben **habe**.	*I'll come as soon as I've finished writing this text.*

■ Separable verbs do not get separated:

Herr Keller glaubt, dass seine Assistentin ihn **anlügt**.	*Herr Keller believes that his assistant is lying to him.*

■ When modal verbs are used in the present perfect tense (**Perfekt**) the conjugated verb comes before all the other verb parts:

Timo erzählt stolz, dass er die Abschiedsrede für den Chef **hat** halten dürfen.	*Timo tells us proudly that he's been allowed to make the farewell speech for the boss.*

The word order for the remaining elements in the clause follows the same rules as in the main clause (see 6, p. 67). There are a great many different types of subordinate clause (**Nebensätze**). Relative clauses (**Relativsätze**) and infinitive clauses (**Infinitivsätze**) will be dealt with separately in the next few chapters because they don't quite conform to the standard pattern. In the case of all other subordinate clauses, the meaning (temporal or causal) is comparatively easy to determine once you know the meaning of the subordinating conjunction involved.

The most important subordinating conjunctions are:

conjunction	main focus of meaning	example
als	temporally simultaneous: point of time in the past	**Als** ich ins Büro kam, war meine Chefin schon da. *When I came into the office, my boss was already there.*
als	comparison	Das Projekt war schneller beendet, **als** wir erwartet hatten. *The project was finished faster than we had expected.*
als ob	unreal comparison	Er tat so, **als ob** er keine Zeit hätte. *He acted as if he had no time.*
bevor	temporal	**Bevor** wir Pläne fürs Wochenende machen, möchte ich noch die Wettervorhersage hören. *Before we make any plans for the weekend, I'd like to hear the weather forecast.*
bis	temporal: end of an action	Wir warten noch, **bis** alle Teammitglieder da sind. *We're waiting until all team members are here.*
da	reason	**Da** Ralf und Anne zu viel Alkohol getrunken hatten, gingen sie lieber zu Fuß nach Hause. *Since Ralf and Anne had drunk too much alcohol, they preferred to walk home.*

damit	aim, purpose	Ich möchte sofort anfangen, **damit** wir pünktlich aufhören können. *I'd like to start immediately so we can finish on time.*
dass	aim, purpose, introduces a statement	Ich glaube, **dass** wir den Termin halten können. *I think that we can meet the deadline.*
nachdem	temporal	**Nachdem** ich im Training gewesen war, ging es mir schon viel besser. *After I had done some training, I felt much better.*
ob	doubt, question, wondering	Ich weiß nicht, **ob** Paul schon zu Hause ist. *I don't know whether Paul is home yet.*
obwohl	limitation	**Obwohl** das Wetter schlecht war, gingen wir spazieren. *Although the weather was bad, we went for a walk.*
seit(dem)	temporal	**Seit** Elena täglich Qigong macht, hat sie keine Kopfschmerzen mehr. *Since Elana has been doing Qi-gong every day, she doesn't have any more headaches.*
weil	reason	Wir kamen zu spät zur Präsentation, **weil** wir im Stau gestanden sind. *We arrived too late for the presentation because we were in a traffic jam.*

conjunction	main focus of meaning	example
wenn	condition	**Wenn** du mal in Köln bist, musst du mich besuchen. *If you're ever in Cologne, you must come and visit me.*
(immer) wenn	temporal repeated action (in the past)	**(Immer) wenn** Maite in Deutschland war, hat sie uns besucht. *Whenever Maite was in Germany, she visited us.*

A subordinate clause can also be introduced by a question word (**Fragewort**). These clauses are called indirect questions (**indirekte Fragesätze**). (Question words see 3.4, p. 45f.). This occurs mainly after a main clause containing verbs like **sagen** *(to say)*, **fragen** *(to ask)* or **wissen** *(to know)*.

Weißt du, **warum** Sylvia so schlechte Laune hat?	*Do you know why Sylvia is in such a bad mood?*
Ich frage mich, **wo** meine Schlüssel sind.	*I wonder where my keys are.*
Hast du verstanden, **was** sie gesagt hat?	*Have you understood what she said?*

Please combine the following sentences using the conjunctions in brackets.

1. Mike ist enttäuscht. Die Vergütung entspricht nicht seinen Vorstellungen. *(weil)*
2. Peer wirkt gelassen. Er macht täglich Joga-Übungen. *(seit)*
3. Lucia spielt seit drei Jahren Gitarre. Sie surft auch gerne im Internet. *(und)*
4. Victor freut sich. Er kann nächste Woche in den Urlaub gehen. *(dass)*
5. Das Seminar fand nicht statt. Es gab zu wenig Teilnehmer. *(da)*
6. Frau Wilice besichtigt das Deutsche Museum. Sie geht auf den Marienplatz. *(oder)*

14.3 Die Relativsätze
Relative Clauses
<u>oder</u> *Sätze, die relativ häufig sind*

Alan: Is that the path we should take? – Peter: It doesn't really matter.
They're both paths that end up back in the car park.

Relative clauses (**Relativsätze**) are introduced by a relative pronoun (**Relativpronomen**). A relative clause tells us more about a noun in the main clause. Normally the relative clause comes directly after the noun it describes.

> *Judith trifft einen Kollegen. Den Kollegen hat sie gestern in der Cafeteria kennen gelernt.*
> main clause (Hauptsatz) + main clause (Hauptsatz)
> *Judith meets a colleague. She met the colleague for the first time yesterday in the cafeteria.*

> *Judith trifft einen Kollegen, **den sie gestern in der Cafeteria kennen gelernt hat**.*
> main clause (Hauptsatz) + relative clause (Relativsatz)
> *Judith meets a colleague whom she met for the first time yesterday in the cafeteria.*

Relative clauses often get inserted in the middle of a main clause:

> *Die Präsentation, **die Frau Ronner gehalten hat**, war sehr gut.*
> *The presentation that Frau Ronner held was very good.*

Apart from a few exceptions, the relative pronouns are identical to the definite article.

	masculine	neuter	feminine	plural
nom.	*der*	*das*	*die*	*die*
acc.	*den*	*das*	*die*	*die*
dat.	*dem*	*dem*	*der*	*denen*
gen.	*dessen*	*dessen*	*deren*	*deren*

 The correct form of the relative pronoun depends on two things. We might say that it faces in two directions.

It is the preceding noun being described in the relative clause that determines the gender (masculine, neuter or feminine) and the number (singular or plural), whereas the verb in the relative clause determines the case (nominative, accusative, dative or genitive).

Der Kollege, **den** ich schon lange kenne, hat heute gekündigt.

My colleague, whom I've known for a long time, handed in his notice today.
accusative, masculine, singular

Morgen kommen die Kunden, **denen** du das Angebot geschickt hast.

Tomorrow those customers you sent the offer to are coming.
dative, plural

Relative pronouns can also occur in combination with prepositions, in which case the preposition comes before the relative pronoun.

Das ist der Rucksack, **mit dem** ich schon die halbe Welt bereist habe.	*That's the rucksack with which I've toured half the world.*
Da drüben ist eine Bäckerei, **in der** ich schon als Kind eingekauft habe.	*Over there is a bakery where I've been a customer since I was a child.*
Wir kaufen eine Fahrkarte, **mit der** wir zu fünft fahren können.	*We'll buy a ticket with which all five of us can travel.*

Relative pronouns in the genitive case replace the possessive article (**Possessivartikel**). No other article is then used with the noun that follows.

Die Kollegin, **deren** Hund immer mit ins Büro kommt, hat diese Woche Urlaub.	*The colleague whose dog always comes with her to the office is on holiday this week.*
(**Ihr Hund** kommt immer mit ins Büro.)	*(Her dog always comes with her to the office.)*

Der Mann, **dessen** Auto du beschädigt hast, ist jetzt hier.	*The man whose car you damaged is here now.*
(Du hast **sein Auto** beschädigt.)	*(You damaged his car.)*

Relative clauses can also refer to pronouns or to complete sentences. In these cases the relative pronoun is **was.**

Das ist alles, **was** ich dazu weiß.	*That's all that I know about it.*
Das Wichtigste, **was** in so einem Fall getan werden sollte, ist ...	*The most important thing that should be done in a case like this is ...*
Ich weiß nicht, **was** ich dazu noch sagen soll.	*I don't know what to say to that.*

14.4 Die Infinitivsätze
Infinitive Clauses
oder *Das ist leicht zu lernen*

Another type of subordinate clause is introduced without a normal conjunction. These are infinitive clauses (**Infinitivsätze**) with **zu.**

zu + infinitive
Infinitive clauses with **zu + infinitive** can be used after certain verbs, nouns or adjectives.

■ Verbs with **zu + infinitive**

Here we have two groups of verbs. In the one group, the main clause and the subordinate clause both have the same subject. By using the **zu +** infinitive construction, we can avoid repetition.

zu + infinitive	alternative construction
Wir versuchen, Ihren Auftrag schnellstmöglich **zu bearbeiten**.	Wir versuchen, dass wir Ihren Auftrag schnellstmöglich bearbeiten.
We're trying to complete your order as quickly as possible.	
Hans meint, immer der Beste **sein zu müssen**.	Hans meint, er muss immer der Beste sein.
Hans believes he always needs to be the best.	
Denk daran, deine Medizin regelmäßig **zu nehmen**!	Denk daran, dass du deine Medizin regelmäßig nimmst.
Remember to take your medicine regularly.	

Other verbs in this group are:

anbieten	*to offer to*
anfangen	*to start to*
aufhören	*to stop*
beabsichtigen	*to intend to*
beginnen	*to begin to*
sich bemühen	*to make an effort to*
beschließen	*to decide to*
sich entschließen	*to decide to*
sich freuen	*to look forward to, be pleased to*
fürchten	*to fear to*
sich gewöhnen an	*to get used to*
glauben	*to believe*
hoffen	*to hope to*
planen	*to plan to*
scheinen	*to seem to*
vergessen	*to forget to*
sich verlassen auf	*to rely on sb. to*
versprechen	*to promise to*
vorhaben	*to intend to*
sich weigern	*to refuse to*

■ In the second group of verbs, the **zu** + **infinitive** construction describes what the object of the sentence does.

> *Meine Freundin hat mich dazu überredet, mit ihr ins Theater* **zu gehen**.
> *My girl-friend has persuaded me to go to the theatre with her.*
>
> *Peter hat Alan eingeladen, bei ihm* **zu wohnen**.
> *Peter has invited Alan to stay at his house.*
>
> *Jana fällt es nicht leicht, auf Schokolade* **zu verzichten**.
> *It's not easy for Jana to do without chocolate.*

Other verbs in this group are:

anbieten	*to offer to*
auffordern	*to ask sb. to*
befehlen	*to order sb. to*
bitten	*to ask sb. to*
bringen zu	*to bring sb. to*
empfehlen	*to recommend sb. to*
erinnern an	*to remind sb. to*
erlauben	*to permit sb. to*
ermöglichen	*to make it possible for sb. to*
gelingen	*to succeed in*
helfen	*to help sb. to*
hindern an	*to prevent sb. from*
raten	*to advise sb. to*
schwer fallen	*to have difficulty in*
verbieten	*to forbid sb. to*
warnen vor	*to warn sb. about*

Verbs with a separable prefix have the **zu** in the middle – between prefix and main stem.

> *Eva freut sich darauf, mit Alan und Peter aus**zu**gehen. (ausgehen)*
> *Eva is looking forward to going out with Alan and Peter.*

*Christa hat ihrer Nachbarin angeboten, für sie ein**zu**kaufen. (einkaufen)*
Christa has offered her neighbour to do her shopping for her.

*Dem Team gelang es, ein sensationelles Angebot aus**zu**arbeiten.*
(ausarbeiten)
The team succeeded in working out a sensational offer.

■ Nouns with **zu** + **infinitive**

*Die Kinder haben keine **Lust**, ihre Zimmer **aufzuräumen**.*
The children don't feel like tidying up their rooms.

*Elisabeth hat die **Absicht**, die Stelle **zu wechseln**.*
Elisabeth intends to change her job.

*Helmut hatte kein **Problem**, sich mit den Leuten in Peru **zu**
verständigen.*
Helmut had no problem in communicating with the people in Peru.

Further nouns followed by **zu** + **infinitive** are:

die Angst	*fear (of)*
die Freude	*joy, pleasure (in)*
die Gelegenheit	*opportunity (to/of)*
der Grund	*reason (to)*
die Möglichkeit	*possibility (of)*
die Mühe	*effort, trouble (to)*
das Problem	*problem (in)*
die Schwierigkeiten	*difficulty (in)*
der Spaß	*fun (in)*
die Zeit	*time (to)*

■ Adjectives and participles with **zu** + **infinitive**

These adjectives or participles normally come after a form of the verb
sein *(to be)* or **finden** *(to find)*.

*Es **ist** gesund, viel Gemüse und Obst **zu essen**.*
It's healthy to eat lots of vegetables and fruit.

> *Viele Leute **finden** es unhöflich, ohne Entschuldigung deutlich zu spät **zu kommen**.*
> *Many people find it impolite to arrive much too late without an apology.*

Further adjectives and participles of this kind are:

bereit	*ready (to)*
entschlossen	*determined (to)*
erlaubt/verboten	*permitted/forbidden (to)*
erfreut	*pleased (to)*
erstaunt	*amazed (to)*
falsch/richtig	*wrong/right (to)*
gewohnt	*accustomed/used (to)*
gut/schlecht	*good/bad (to)*
interessant/uninteressant	*interesting/uninteresting (to)*
nötig/unnötig	*necessary/unnecessary (to)*
praktisch/unpraktisch	*practical/impractical (to)*
stolz	*proud (to)*
überzeugt	*convinced (about)*
wichtig/unwichtig	*important/unimportant (to)*

■ ***um + zu* + infinitive**

Sentences with ***um + zu* + infinitive** express a purpose or an aim in the same way as subordinate clauses with the conjunction ***damit***. If the subject of the main clause and the subordinate clause are identical, we can use the ***um + zu* + infinitive** construction. Otherwise we have to use ***damit***.

um + zu + infinitive	*damit*
*Wir haben in dieser Sitzung keine Zeit, **um** über so ein Thema **zu diskutieren**.*	*Wir haben diese Sitzung nicht einberufen, **damit** Sie dieses unwichtige Thema diskutieren.*
We don't have time in this meeting to discuss such a topic.	*We haven't called this meeting so that you can discuss this unimportant topic.*

Paula ist gekommen, **um** uns beim Umzug **zu helfen**.

Paula has come to help us with the move.

Paula ist gekommen, **damit** Laura die Arbeit nicht allein machen muss.

Paula has come so that Laura doesn't have to do the work on her own.

Sina arbeitet im Kino, **um** ihr Taschengeld **aufzubessern**.

Sina is working at the cinema to earn some more pocket money.

Sina arbeitet im Kino, **damit** die ganze Familie Freikarten bekommt.

Sina is working at the cinema so her whole family can get free tickets.

Here, too, separable verbs have the **zu** in the middle.

Leo ist auf den Markt gegangen, **um** ein**zu**kaufen.
Leo has gone to the market to do some shopping.

Wir sind ins Naturkundemuseum gegangen, **um** uns die Saurierskelette an**zu**sehen.
We went to the Natural History Museum to see the dinosaur skeletons.

15 Die Wortbildung
Word Formation

oder

Aus zwei mach vier
Making four out of two

Peter: See that barrel of beer over there? In a minute the Lord Mayor will come and tap it and draw the first glass of beer. Then the Oktoberfest is officially open. – Alan: Do they have wine here, too? I'm a great wine-drinker. – Eva: Honestly, this isn't a wine festival, you know.

Whether it's beer or wine you prefer, one thing you'll like about German is the fact that you can increase your vocabulary by using the rules of word formation. New composite words can be created by combining two or more single ones or by adding prefixes or suffixes. This happens all the time and new combinations can occur daily.

If you come across a long complicated-looking word that you don't understand, it often helps if you split it up into its constituent parts. You'll probably understand each of these more easily. Then read these single elements in reverse order and the meaning of the whole word will become clear.

Thus a **Schweine/hals/braten** is a **Braten** (*roast*) from the **Hals** (*neck*) of a **Schwein** (*pig*) and **Semmel/knödel** are **Knödel** (*dumplings*) made from **Semmeln** (Bavarian word for *bread rolls*).

15.1 Die Komposition
Composing New Words
<u>oder</u> *Fassbier und Flaschenwein*

No matter how many elements the compound word (**Kompositum**) has, it is always the last element that determines what kind of word it is. In the case of nouns, the last element determines the gender. The preceding elements tell us more about it. They define the basic word.

> **der Flaschenwein**
> defining word + basic word
> *wine from a bottle (and not from a barrel)*
>
> **die Weinflasche**
> defining word + basic word
> *a bottle of wine (and not a glass)*

The meaning of a compound word does not necessarily correspond with the meaning of its constituent parts. A **Kindergarten** is not a **Garten** (*garden*) for **Kinder** (*children*), but a kind of school for very young children.

Word composition like this occurs most often with nouns, but can also take place with other kinds of words.

■ **Noun + Noun**

> die Steuer + **der** Berater = **der** Steuerberater
> *tax + advisor = tax advisor*
>
> die Liebe + **der** Kummer = **der** Liebeskummer
> *love + worries = trouble with your love-life*
>
> der Traum + **der** Job = **der** Traumjob
> *dream + job = dream job*

■ **Adjective + Noun**

> rot + **der** Wein = **der** Rotwein
> *red + wine = red wine*
>
> groß + **die** Stadt = **die** Großstadt
> *big + town = city*
>
> weich + **das** Ei = **das** Weichei
> *soft + egg = softy, weakling*

■ **Noun + Adjective**

> das Vitamin + reich = vitaminreich
> *vitamin + rich = rich in vitamins*
>
> die Umwelt + schonend = umweltschonend
> *environment + treating with care = environmentally friendly*
>
> das Bild + schön = bildschön
> *picture + beautiful = pretty as a picture*
>
> die Medien + wirksam = medienwirksam
> *media + effective = to great effect in the media*

■ **Verb + Noun**

schlafen + **das** *Zimmer* = **das** *Schlafzimmer*
sleep + room = bedroom

tanzen + **die** *Schuhe* = **die** *Tanzschuhe*
dance + shoes = dancing shoes

boxen + **die** *Handschuhe* = **die** *Boxhandschuhe*
box + gloves = boxing-gloves

■ **Preposition + Noun**

vor + **der** *Vertrag* = **der** *Vorvertrag*
before + contract = provisional contract

nach + **die** *Sicht* = **die** *Nachsicht*
after + sight = tolerance

innen + **die** *Politik* = **die** *Innenpolitik*
inner + politics = home affairs

■ **Adjective + Adjective**

dunkel + rot = dunkelrot
dark + red = dark red

hell + blond = hellblond
light + blond = light-blond

■ **Adverb + Verb**

wieder + sehen = wiedersehen
again + see = meet again

Often several of the above word types are combined. In principle anything is possible, provided you can remember at the end of the word what the beginning was. Examples:

die Mit/fahr/gelegenheit	*chance of a lift*
die Mit/wohn/zentrale	*flat sharing agency*
lila/blass/blau	*pinkish pale blue*
der Vor/stands/vor/sitzende	*Chairman of the Board, Chief Executive*
die Mit/arbeiter/versammlung	*staff meeting*

And, of course, the now very famous but tongue-in-cheek example:

Donaudampfschifffahrtsgesellschaftskapitänskajütentürschloss
The lock on the cabin door of the captain from the Danube steam-ship company

A lot of compound nouns refuse to fit together without a little help. They need something to seal the join, a kind of hinge:

die Arbeit + der Markt = der Arbeit**s**markt
work + market = labour market

der Aufwand + die Entschädigung = die Aufwand**s**entschädigung
effort + compensation = compensation for work involved

Quite a lot of compounds make use of the plural rather than the singular.

die Aprikosen (plural) + die Marmelade = die Aprikosenmarmelade
(You need more than one apricot.)
apricots + jam = apricot jam

die Kinder (plural) + der Garten = der Kindergarten
(There's always more than one child.)
children + garden = kindergarten
(English and German use the same word)

EXERCISE 21	Please form compound words from the following and then add the correct form of the definite article.

1. Baum + Gummi ___ _____
2. Ordner + Ring ___ _____
3. Papier + Drucker ___ _____
4. Schalter + Licht ___ _____
5. Läufer + schnell ___ _____
6. Wohnung + Markt ___ _____
7. über + Bevölkerung ___ _____
8. Tasche + Handy ___ _____
9. nass + Schnee ___ _____
10. blau + hell ___ _____
11. Abend + vor ___ _____
12. Zeitung + Abonnement ___ _____

15.2 Die Derivation
Deriving New Words
oder *Verständlich und lernbar*

We can derive new words by adding a prefix or a suffix to an existing basic element. The kind of word can vary. In the case of verbs, the infinitive ending often disappears.

> *programmieren – der Programmier**er** – die Programmier**erin***
> *to program – male programmer – female programmer*
>
> *frei + **-heit** = die Freiheit*
> *free – freedom*
>
> *fahren – die Fahrt*
> *to travel – journey*
>
> *bewegen + **-ung** = die Bewegung*
> *to move – movement*

der Sommer + **-lich** = *sommerlich*
summer – summery

der Frühling + **-(s)haft** = *frühlingshaft*
spring – spring-like

be + *arbeiten* = *bearbeiten*
to work – to work on something

■ Prefixes are often used with verbs, e.g. **ankommen** (*to arrive*), **durchlesen** (*to read through*), **wiederholen** (*to repeat*). See 7.3, p. 79ff. With nouns and adjectives we very often find the prefixes **in-** and **un-**. They turn the noun into its negative form or its opposite.

das Unglück (kein *Glück*)	*calamity, misfortune (no luck)*
unglücklich (nicht *glücklich* usw.)	*unhappy (not happy)*
der Unsinn	*nonsense*
unsinnig	*nonsensical, silly*
unfreundlich	*unfriendly, rude*
die Inkompetenz	*incompetence*
inkompetent	*incompetent*
insolvent	*insolvent, bankrupt*
die Instabilität	*instability*

■ Suffixes are used to form new nouns or adjectives. As a result, new words are formed on the basis of other nouns, verbs or adjectives. In the case of nouns, the suffix will determine the gender of the new noun (see 2.1, p. 23ff.).

gesund + **-heit** = *die Gesundheit*
healthy – health

fröhlich + **-keit** = *die Fröhlichkeit*
good-humoured – good-humour

bearbeiten + **-ung** = *die Bearbeitung*
to work on something – the actual work itself

der Wunsch + **-los** = wunschlos
wish – without a wish (completely satisfied)

leben + **-haft** = lebhaft
to live – lively

der Wind + **-ig** = windig
wind – windy

EXERCISE 22 Please add the missing prefixes and suffixes.

1. Simons Katze ist _____ laufen.
2. Herr Franklin muss noch _____ checken.
3. Marilyn ist krank und sollte sich daher _____ decken.
4. Die Reisefrei_____ war als wichtiger Fortschritt zu betrachten.
5. Das Bungeejumping sieht gefähr_____ aus.
6. Frau Setlur macht einen jugend_____ Eindruck.
7. Wir müssen das Geschenk _____ packen.
8. Sollen wir Sie das Stück _____ nehmen?
9. Auf dieses Angebot werden Sie bestimmt noch _____ kommen.
10. Die Freund_____ mit Jenny war mir viel wert.
11. Die Assistent_____ stellte das Projekt fertig.
12. Wir hoffen, dass Sie jetzt nicht mehr sprach_____ sind!

Now that we've made your mouth water and given you an appetite for our language, the Oktoberfest and lots of other nice things, it's time to say goodbye and wish you every success for your future German studies. Have lots of fun!

Anhang
Appendix

Unregelmäßige und gemischte Verben
German Irregular and Mixed Verbs

The most important irregular and mixed verbs are listed alphabetically in the following tables. Mixed verbs are marked with an *.
All verbs are listed in groups according to the vowel changes they undergo in their different tenses (see 9.2).

infinitive	present tense (Präsens, 3. Person Singular)	past simple (Präteritum)	present perfect (Perfekt)		translation
A – B – A					
blasen	bläst	blies	hat	geblasen	*to blow*
braten	brät	briet	hat	gebraten	*to roast*
empfangen	empfängt	empfing	hat	empfangen	*to receive*
fallen	fällt	fiel	ist	gefallen	*to fall*
fangen	fängt	fing	hat	gefangen	*to catch*
geraten	gerät	geriet	ist	geraten	*to fall/ get into*
hängen	hängt	hing	hat	gehangen	*to hang*
halten	hält	hielt	hat	gehalten	*to stop, hold*
lassen	lässt	ließ	hat	gelassen	*to let, leave, stop*
raten	rät	riet	hat	geraten	*to guess*
schlafen	schläft	schlief	hat	geschlafen	*to sleep*
laufen	läuft	lief	ist	gelaufen	*to run*
heißen	heißt	hieß	hat	geheißen	*to be called*
stoßen	stößt	stieß	hat	gestoßen	*to push, knock*
rufen	ruft	rief	hat	gerufen	*to call*
backen	bäckt (backt)	buk (backte)	hat	gebacken	*to bake*

infinitive	present tense (Präsens, 3. Person Singular)	past simple (Präteritum)	present perfect (Perfekt)		translation
fahren	fährt	fuhr	hat/ist	gefahren	to drive, travel
graben	gräbt	grub	hat	gegraben	to dig
laden	lädt	lud	hat	geladen	to load
schaffen	schafft	schuf	hat	geschaffen	to create, do
schlagen	schlägt	schlug	hat	geschlagen	to hit, beat
tragen	trägt	trug	hat	getragen	to carry, to wear
wachsen	wächst	wuchs	ist	gewachsen	to grow
waschen	wäscht	wusch	hat	gewaschen	to wash
essen	isst	aß	hat	gegessen	to eat (of people)
fressen	frisst	fraß	hat	gefressen	to eat (of animals)
geben	gibt	gab	hat	gegeben	to give
geschehen	geschieht	geschah	ist	geschehen	to happen
lesen	liest	las	hat	gelesen	to read
messen	misst	maß	hat	gemessen	to measure
sehen	sieht	sah	hat	gesehen	to see
treten	tritt	trat	hat/ist	getreten	to step, kick
vergessen	vergisst	vergaß	hat	vergessen	to forget

A – B – B

*brennen	brennt	brannte	hat	gebrannt	to burn
*bringen	bringt	brachte	hat	gebracht	to bring, fetch, take
*denken	denkt	dachte	hat	gedacht	to think
*kennen	kennt	kannte	hat	gekannt	to know (be acquainted)
*nennen	nennt	nannte	hat	genannt	to name, call
*rennen	rennt	rannte	ist	gerannt	to run, race

infinitive	present tense (Präsens, 3. Person Singular)	past simple (Präteritum)	present perfect (Perfekt)		translation
*senden	sendet	sandte (sendete)	hat	gesandt (gesendet)	to send
stehen	steht	stand	hat/ist	gestanden	to stand
beweisen	beweist	bewies	hat	bewiesen	to prove
bleiben	bleibt	blieb	ist	geblieben	to stay, remain
gedeihen	gedeiht	gedieh	ist	gediehen	to flourish
leihen	leiht	lieh	hat	geliehen	to lend
meiden	meidet	mied	hat	gemieden	to avoid
preisen	preist	pries	hat	gepriesen	to praise
reiben	reibt	rieb	hat	gerieben	to rub
scheiden	scheidet	schied	hat/ist	geschieden	to separate
scheinen	scheint	schien	hat	geschienen	to seem, to shine
schmeißen	schmeißt	schmiss	hat	geschmissen	to throw, hurl
schreiben	schreibt	schrieb	hat	geschrieben	to write
schreien	schreit	schrie	hat	geschrien	to scream, cry
schweigen	schweigt	schwieg	hat	geschwiegen	to stay silent
steigen	steigt	stieg	ist	gestiegen	to climb, to rise
treiben	treibt	trieb	hat	getrieben	to drive, drift, do
verzeihen	verzeiht	verzieh	hat	verziehen	to forgive
weisen	weist	wies	hat	gewiesen	to direct, show
beißen	beißt	biss	hat	gebissen	to bite
gleichen	gleicht	glich	hat	geglichen	to be similar to, same as
gleiten	gleitet	glitt	ist	geglitten	to glide

infinitive	present tense (Präsens, 3. Person Singular)	past simple (Präteritum)	present perfect (Perfekt)		translation
greifen	greift	griff	hat	gegriffen	to grab, grip
kneifen	kneift	kniff	hat	gekniffen	to pinch
leiden	leidet	litt	hat	gelitten	to suffer
pfeifen	pfeift	pfiff	hat	gepfiffen	to whistle
reißen	reißt	riss	hat/ist	gerissen	to tear, break
reiten	reitet	ritt	hat/ist	geritten	to ride
schleichen	schleicht	schlich	ist	geschlichen	to slide, slip, slink
schneiden	schneidet	schnitt	hat	geschnitten	to cut
schreiten	schreitet	schritt	ist	geschritten	to step
streichen	streicht	strich	hat	gestrichen	to spread, paint, cut out
streiten	streitet	stritt	hat	gestritten	to quarrel, argue
weichen	weicht	wich	ist	gewichen	to give way, move
heben	hebt	hob	hat	gehoben	to lift, raise
biegen	biegt	bog	hat/ist	gebogen	to bend
bieten	bietet	bot	hat	geboten	to offer
erwägen	erwägt	erwog	hat	erwogen	to consider
fliegen	fliegt	flog	hat/ist	geflogen	to fly
fliehen	flieht	floh	ist	geflohen	to flee
fließen	fließt	floss	ist	geflossen	to flow
frieren	friert	fror	hat	gefroren	to freeze
genießen	genießt	genoss	hat	genossen	to enjoy
gießen	gießt	goss	hat	gegossen	to pour
kriechen	kriecht	kroch	ist	gekrochen	to crawl
riechen	riecht	roch	hat	gerochen	to smell
schieben	schiebt	schob	hat	geschoben	to push
schießen	schießt	schoss	hat/ist	geschossen	to shoot

infinitive	present tense (*Präsens, 3. Person Singular*)	past simple (*Präteritum*)	present perfect (*Perfekt*)		translation
schließen	schließt	schloss	hat	geschlossen	to close
sprießen	sprießt	spross	ist	gesprossen	to sprout
verlieren	verliert	verlor	hat	verloren	to lose
wiegen	wiegt	wog	hat	gewogen	to weigh
ziehen	zieht	zog	hat/ist	gezogen	to pull
*wissen	weiß	wusste	hat	gewusst	to know (facts)
*können	kann	konnte	hat	gekonnt	to be able (can)
*mögen	mag	mochte	hat	gemocht	to like
betrügen	betrügt	betrog	hat	betrogen	to deceive
lügen	lügt	log	hat	gelogen	to lie
*müssen	muss	musste	hat	gemusst	to have to (must)
*dürfen	darf	durfte	hat	gedurft	to be allowed to (may)

A – B – C

infinitive	present	past simple	present perfect		translation
befehlen	befiehlt	befahl	hat	befohlen	to order, instruct
bergen	birgt	barg	hat	geborgen	to save, rescue, recover
bewerben	bewirbt	bewarb	hat	beworben	to apply (for)
brechen	bricht	brach	hat/ist	gebrochen	to break
empfehlen	empfiehlt	empfahl	hat	empfohlen	to recommend
erschrecken	erschrickt	erschrak	hat/ist	erschrocken	to frighten, be frightened
gelten	gilt	galt	hat	gegolten	to be valid, to count

infinitive	present tense (Präsens, 3. Person Singular)	past simple (Präteritum)	present perfect (Perfekt)		translation
helfen	hilft	half	hat	geholfen	to help
nehmen	nimmt	nahm	hat	genommen	to take
sprechen	spricht	sprach	hat	gesprochen	to speak
stechen	sticht	stach	hat	gestochen	to sting, bite, stab
stehlen	stiehlt	stahl	hat	gestohlen	to steal
sterben	stirbt	starb	ist	gestorben	to die
treffen	trifft	traf	hat	getroffen	to meet, to hit
verderben	verdirbt	verdarb	hat/ist	verdorben	to spoil
werben	wirbt	warb	hat	geworben	to advertise
werfen	wirft	warf	hat	geworfen	to throw
beginnen	beginnt	begann	hat	begonnen	to begin
gewinnen	gewinnt	gewann	hat	gewonnen	to win
schwimmen	schwimmt	schwamm	hat/ist	geschwommen	to swim
bitten	bittet	bat	hat	gebeten	to ask, to request
liegen	liegt	lag	hat	gelegen	to lie (position)
sitzen	sitzt	saß	hat/ist	gesessen	to sit
binden	bindet	band	hat	gebunden	to bind, tie
dringen	dringt	drang	ist	gedrungen	to push through
empfinden	empfindet	empfand	hat	empfunden	to feel
finden	findet	fand	hat	gefunden	to find
gelingen	gelingt	gelang	ist	gelungen	to succeed
klingen	klingt	klang	hat	geklungen	to sound
misslingen	misslingt	misslang	ist	misslungen	to fail
ringen	ringt	rang	hat	gerungen	to wrestle
schlingen	schlingt	schlang	hat	geschlungen	to tie, wrap

infinitive	present tense (*Präsens, 3. Person Singular*)	past simple (*Präteritum*)	present perfect (*Perfekt*)		translation
schwinden	schwindet	schwand	ist	geschwunden	*to fade, wane*
schwingen	schwingt	schwang	hat	geschwungen	*to swing*
singen	singt	sang	hat	gesungen	*to sing*
sinken	sinkt	sank	ist	gesunken	*to sink*
springen	springt	sprang	ist	gesprungen	*to jump*
stinken	stinkt	stank	hat	gestunken	*to stink*
trinken	trinkt	trank	hat	getrunken	*to drink*
zwingen	zwingt	zwang	hat	gezwungen	*to force*

andere Verben

*haben	hat	hatte	hat	gehabt	*to have*
sein	ist	war	ist	gewesen	*to be*
*sollen	soll	sollte	hat	gesollt	*to be supposed to*
*wollen	will	wollte	hat	gewollt	*to want*
tun	tut	tat	hat	getan	*to do*
kommen	kommt	kam	ist	gekommen	*to come*
werden	wird	wurde	ist	geworden	*to become*
gehen	geht	ging	ist	gegangen	*to go*

Die wichtigsten Dativ-Verben
The Most Important Verbs Taking the Dative

Verbs with Dative only

ähneln	*to look like, be similar to*
auffallen	*to be noticeable (to sb.)*
antworten	*to answer*
befehlen	*to order, instruct*
begegnen	*to meet*
beistehen	*to stand by, support sb.*
danken	*to thank*
einfallen	*to occur (to sb.)*
entgegnen	*to reply, retort, counter*
erscheinen	*to appear*
erwidern	*to reply*
fehlen	*to miss, be missing*
folgen	*to follow*
gefallen	*to please*
gehören	*to belong*
gehorchen	*to obey*
gelingen	*to succeed*
genügen	*to satisfy, be enough*
glauben	*to believe (sb.)*
gratulieren	*to congratulate*
helfen	*to help*
missfallen	*to displease*
misslingen	*to fail*
sich nähern	*to approach*
nützen	*to be useful*
passen	*to suit*
raten	*to advise*
schaden	*to harm, damage*
schmecken	*to taste*
vertrauen	*to trust*
verzeihen	*to forgive*

(aus)weichen	*to avoid*
widersprechen	*to contradict*
zuhören	*to listen*
zureden	*to persuade, encourage*
zusagen	*to accept, confirm, approve*
zuschauen	*to watch*
zusehen	*to watch*
zustimmen	*to agree*
zuwenden	*to devote (to), bestow (on)*

Verbs with Dative and Accusative

anvertrauen	*to entrust sb. with sth.*
beantworten	*to answer sb. sth.*
beweisen	*to prove sth. to sb.*
borgen	*to borrow, lend sb. sth.*
bringen	*to bring, take, fetch sb. sth.*
empfehlen	*to recommend sb. sth.*
entwenden	*to remove, steal sth. from sb.*
entziehen	*to withdraw sth. from sb.*
erlauben	*to permit, allow sb. sth.*
erzählen	*to tell, narrate sb. sth.*
geben	*to give sb. sth.*
leihen	*to lend sb. sth.*
liefern	*to deliver sth. to sb.*
melden	*to report sth. to sb.*
mitteilen	*to inform sb. of sth.*
nehmen	*to take sb. sth.*
rauben	*to rob sb. of sth.*
sagen	*to say sth. to sb.*
schenken	*to give sb. sth. (as a present)*
schicken	*to send sb. sth.*
schreiben	*to write sb. sth.*
schulden	*to owe sb. sth.*
senden	*to send sb. sth.*
stehlen	*to steal sth. from sb.*
überlassen	*to relinquisch, let sb. have sth.*

verbieten	*to forbid sb. sth.*
verschweigen	*to keep quiet about sth. to sb.*
versprechen	*to promise sb. sth.*
verweigern	*to refuse sb. sth.*
verzeihen	*to forgive sb. sth.*
vorlesen	*to read sth. out loud to sb.*
vorwerfen	*to accuse. blame sb. of sth.*
wegnehmen	*to take sth away from sb.*
zeigen	*to show sb. sth.*

Verben mit festen Präpositionen
Verbs with Fixed Prepositions

abhängen	von + D(ativ)	*to depend on*
sich amüsieren	über + A(kkusativ)	*to be amused about*
achten	auf + A	*to pay attention to*
anfangen	mit + D	*to begin with*
ankommen	auf + A	*to depend on*
antworten	auf + A	*to answer*
sich ärgern	über + A	*to be annoyed about*
aufhören	mit + D	*to stop doing*
aufpassen	auf + A	*to look after*
sich aufregen	über + A	*to get excited about*
ausgeben	für + A	*to spend on*
sich bedanken	bei + D; für + A	*to thank sb. for*
beginnen	mit + D	*to begin with*
sich bemühen	um + A	*to try to get/take trouble over*
berichten	über + A	*to report on*
sich beschäftigen	mit + D	*to busy oneself with*
sich beschränken	auf + A	*to limit oneself to*
sich beschweren	bei + D; über + A	*to complain to sb. about*
bestehen	aus + D	*to consist of*
bestellen	für + A	*to order for*
bestrafen	für + A	*to punish for*
sich beteiligen	an + D	*to tke part in/have a share in*
sich bewerben	um + A	*to apply for*
sich beziehen	auf + A	*to refer to*
bitten	um + A	*to ask for*
brauchen	zu + D	*to need to*
danken	für + A	*to thank for*
denken	an + A	*to think of*
diskutieren	über + A	*to discuss, talk about*
einladen	zu + D	*to invite to*
sich entscheiden	für + A	*to decide on*
sich entschließen	zu + D	*to decide to*
sich entschuldigen	bei + D; für + A	*to apologise to sb. for*
erfahren	durch + A	*to learn from/through*

sich erholen	von + D	*to recover from*
sich erinnern	an + A	*to remember*
erkennen	an + D	*to recognise in*
sich erkundigen	nach + D	*to enquire about*
erzählen	von + D	*to tell (a story) about*
fehlen	an + D	*to be missing*
fragen	nach + D	*to ask after/about*
sich freuen	auf + D	*to look forward to*
sich freuen	über + A	*to be pleased about*
führen	zu + D	*to lead to*
gehen	um + A	*to involve*
gehören	zu + D	*to belong to*
sich gewöhnen	an + A	*to get used to*
glauben	an + A	*to believe in*
gratulieren	zu + D	*to congratulate on*
halten	für + A	*to consider to be*
halten	von + D	*to have an opinion of/on*
sich halten	an + A	*to comply with*
handeln	von + D	*to involve, have to do with*
helfen	bei + D	*to help in*
hindern	an + D	*to prevent from*
hinweisen	auf + A	*to point out*
hoffen	auf + A	*to hope for*
hören	von + D	*to hear from/about*
sich informieren	über + A	*to find out about*
sich interessieren	für + A	*to be interested in*
interessiert sein	an + D	*to be interested in*
sich konzentrieren	auf + A	*to concentrate on*
kämpfen	für + A	*to fight for*
klagen	über + A	*to complain about*
kommen	zu + D	*to come to*
sich kümmern	um + A	*to take care of*
lachen	über + A	*to laugh at/about*
leiden	an + D	*to suffer from*
leiden	unter + D	*to suffer from, have problems with*
liegen	an + D	*to be due to (cause)*
nachdenken	über + A	*to think about*
profitieren	von + D	*to profit from*

protestieren	gegen + A	to protest against
rechnen	mit + D	to reckon on/with
reden	über + A	to talk about
reden	von + D	to talk of
riechen	nach + D	to smell of
sagen	über + A	to say about
sagen	zu + D	to say to
schicken	zu + D	to send to
schmecken	nach + D	to taste of
schreiben	an + A	to write to
sich schützen	vor + D	to protect oneself from
sehen	von + D	to see of
sein	für + A	to be for
sein	gegen + A	to be against
senden	an + A	to send to
sorgen	für + A	to care for, look after
sprechen	mit + D; über + A	to speak to sb. about
sterben	an + D	to die of
suchen	nach + D	to look for
teilnehmen	an + D	to take part in
telefonieren	mit + D	to telephone sb.
träumen	von + D	to dream of
sich trennen	von + D	to part from/with
sich überzeugen	von + D	to convince oneself about
sich unterhalten	mit + D; über + A	to have a conversation with sb. about
sich unterscheiden	von + D	to differ from
sich verabreden	für + A; mit + D	to arrange to meet on/at … with
sich verabschieden	von + D	to say goodbye to
verbinden	mit + D	to connect with
vergleichen	mit + D	to compare with/to
sich verlassen	auf + A	to rely on
sich verlieben	in + A	to fall in love with
sich verständigen	mit + D	to communicate with
verstehen	von + D	to understand about
sich verstehen	mit + D	to get on well with
sich vorbereiten	auf + A	to prepare to/for

sich vorstellen	*bei + D*	*to have an interview with*
warnen	*vor + D*	*to warn about*
warten	*auf + A*	*to wait for*
sich wenden	*an + A*	*to turn to*
werden	*zu + D*	*to become*
wissen	*von + D*	*to know of*
sich wundern	*über + A*	*to wonder about*
zweifeln	*an + D*	*to have doubts about*
zwingen	*zu + D*	*to force, compel to*

Grammatische Fachbegriffe
Grammatical Terms

Accusative (acc.)	Der Akkusativ
Active (voice)	Das Aktiv
Adjective	Das Adjektiv
Adverb	Das Adverb
Article	Der Artikel
Auxiliary verb	Das Hilfsverb
Case	Der Kasus
Comparative	Der Komparativ
Compound word	Das Kompositum
Conjugation	Die Konjugation
Conjunction	Die Konjunktion
Dative (dat.)	Der Dativ
Declension (of nouns, articles, pronouns and adjectives)	Die Deklination (von Substantiven, Artikel, Pronomen und Adjektiven)
Definite article	Der bestimmte Artikel
Demonstrative pronoun	Das Demonstrativpronomen
Direct speech	Die direkte Rede
Feminine	Feminin
Future tense	Das Futur
Future perfect tense	Das Futur II
Gender	Das Genus
Genitive (gen.)	Der Genitiv
Imperative	Der Imperativ
Indefinite article	Der unbestimmte Artikel
Indefinite pronoun	Das Indefinitpronomen
Indicative	Der Indikativ
Indirect speech	Die indirekte Rede
Infinitive	Der Infinitiv
Infinitive clause	Der Infinitivsatz
Interrogative pronoun	Das Interrogativpronomen
Irregular verb	Das starke Verb
Konjunktiv s. unter "Subjunctive"	Der Konjunktiv
Main clause	Der Hauptsatz
Manner	Modalform

Masculine	Maskulin
Mixed verb	Das Mischverb
Modal particle	Die Modalpartikel
Modal verb	Das Modalverb
Mood	Der Modus
Neuter	Neutrum
Nominative (nom.)	Der Nominativ
Noun	Das Substantiv
Number	Der Numerus
Object	Das Objekt
Past participle	Das Partizip Perfekt (Partizip II)
Passive (voice)	Das Passiv
Past subjunctive	Der Konjunktiv II (= Konjunktiv Imperfekt)
Past perfect	Das Plusquamperfekt
Past tense/Simple past	Das Präteritum
Personal pronoun	Das Personalpronomen
Plural	Der Plural
Positive	Der Positiv
Possessive article	Der Possessivartikel
Possessive pronoun	Das Possessivpronomen
Prefix	Das Präfix
Preposition	Die Präposition
Present participle	Das Partizip Präsens (Partizip I)
Present perfect	Das Perfekt
Present subjunctive	Der Konjunktiv I (= Konjunktiv Präsens)
Present tense	Das Präsens
Pronoun	Das Pronomen
Reciprocal pronouns	Das Reziprokpronomen
Reflexive	Reflexiv
Reflexive pronoun	Das Reflexivpronomen
Regular verb	Das schwache Verb
Relative clause	Der Relativsatz
Relative pronoun	Das Relativpronomen
Singular	Der Singular

Subject	Das Subjekt
Subjunctive s. auch unter: Present subjunctive und Past subjunctive	Der Konjunktiv
Subordinating conjunction	Die Subjunktion
Subordinate clause	Der Nebensatz
Superlative	Der Superlativ
Tense	Das Tempus
Umlaut	Der Umlaut
Verb	Das Verb
Vowel	Der Vokal
Zero article	Der Nullartikel
Zustandspassiv	Das Zustandspassiv

Lösungen zu den Übungen
Key to the Exercises

Exercise 1

1. Herr Blum hat **eine** neue Assistentin. **Die** Assistentin kommt aus Berlin.
2. Herr Bodet ist Marketingdirektor.
3. **Das** alte Computerprogramm war langsamer.
4. Frau Radwan fährt heute mit ihrem Kollegen nach Hamburg.
5. Herr Stix ist Österreicher.
6. **Der** Kopierer ist schon wieder kaputt.
7. Tina macht einen Sprachkurs in Spanien.
8. Während der Besprechung gab es nur Kekse.
9. **Die** Kolleginnen im Call-Center müssen Geduld aufbringen.
10. Die Sekretärin buchte **einen** Flug nach Paris.
11. **Die** Teamassistentin bestellt **den** Toner und **das** Papier.
12. Frau Kolar fand im Besprechungszimmer **ein** Handy.
13. Herr Hundt hat **einen** neuen Kollegen. **Der** Kollege kommt aus Leipzig.
14. Frau Danz schreibt **einen** Bericht. **Der** Bericht muss morgen fertig sein.
15. Hat **die** Firma **eine** Webseite? Nein, die Firma hat wirklich **keine** Webseite.

Exercise 2

die Freundschaft, **das** Häuschen, **der** Zwilling, **der** Katalysator, **die** Freiheit, **die** Erziehung, **der** Mechanismus, **die** Schülerin, **die** Musik, **das** Brüderlein, **die** Verspätung, **die** Station, **der** Präsident, **die** Biologie, **die** Kleinigkeit, **der** Fabrikant, **der** König, **das** Radio, **die** Verwandtschaft, **das** Visum, **der** Winter, **der** Chef, **das** Instrument, **die** Druckerei, **die** Universität, **das** Mädchen, **das** Sortiment

Exercise 3

1. die Reise	die Reisen
2. das Video	die Videos
3. der Brief	die Briefe
4. die Kassette	die Kassetten
5. das Brötchen	die Brötchen

6. der Tag	die Tage
7. der Bohrer	die Bohrer
8. die Brille	die Brillen
9. das Motorrad	die Motorräder
10. der Stift	die Stifte
11. der Trainee	die Trainees
12. das Jahr	die Jahre
13. die Sekretärin	die Sekretärinnen
14. das Zimmer	die Zimmer
15. der Drucker	die Drucker

E x e r c i s e 4

1. Die Verkäuferin half dem **Kunden** bei der Suche.
2. Das ist mein **Kollege** Martin.
3. Eine Redewendung besagt: Der **Glaube** versetzt Berge.
4. Herr Techmer hilft dem **Praktikanten** bei der Seminararbeit.
5. Die Richterin glaubt dem **Zeugen**.
6. Die Journalistin interviewt einen **Experten**.
7. Ich muss mich bei dem **Lieferanten** beschweren.
8. Der Höhepunkt ist die Ansprache des **Bundespräsidenten**.
9. Die Fahndung nach dem **Terroristen** läuft auf Hochtouren.
10. Darüber machten wir uns keine **Gedanken**.

E x e r c i s e 5

1. Mark arbeitet an einer neuen Homepage. Seit **er** sich mit Webdesign beschäftigt, sieht man **ihn** nur selten beim Joggen.
2. Julie sucht einen Job als Programmiererin. **Sie** hat auf diesem Gebiet bereits Erfahrungen gesammelt.
3. Carlos geht ein Jahr nach Deutschland, um seine Sprachkenntnisse zu verbessern. Es wird **ihm** dort bestimmt gefallen.
4. Hast **du** daran gedacht, dass Andrea heute eine Stelle als Praktikantin antritt? **Du** solltest **ihr** viel Glück wünschen!
5. Herr Smith, ich danke **Ihnen**, dass **Sie** gekommen sind. Ist **Ihre** Frau auch dabei?
6. Elena hat noch verschiedene Prüfungen zu absolvieren. Wir werden **ihr** dabei helfen.
7. Andrew, soll ich **dich** bei **deiner** Freundin abholen?
8. **Ich** werde **mich** noch per E-Mail mit Frau Miller in Verbindung setzen.

Exercise 6a

1. Wer hat **diesen** Film mit Julia Roberts gesehen?
2. **Dieser** CD-Player gehört Luca.
3. Wir wussten nicht, wie **dieses** Diktiergerät funktionierte.
4. **Dieses** Verhalten gab mir zu denken.
5. Sie sollten **diesem** Vorfall keine Beachtung schenken.
6. Ich habe **dieses** Wort noch nie gehört.
7. **Diese** Fragen wurden mit Hilfe des Internets gelöst.
8. Carla wird **diese** Wohnung in Hamburg mieten.

Exercise 6b

Wir suchen Möbel für unsere Wohnung in Deutschland und finden in einem Einrichtungshaus …

1. … einen Küchentisch. – **Dieser** ist leider zu groß für unsere Küche.
2. … einen Einbauschrank. – **Dieser** gefällt uns ausgezeichnet.
3. … eine Eckbank. – **Diese** ist uns zu teuer.
4. … Stühle für die Essecke. – **Diese** können wir auf jeden Fall gebrauchen.
5. … einen Schreibtisch. – **Dieser** ist etwas zu klein.
6. … eine Wohnzimmerlampe. – **Diese** sollten wir gleich mitnehmen.

Exercise 7

1. Lars kauft **sich** ein neues Sweatshirt.
2. Yukis Bemerkungen ärgerten **mich**.
3. Ich freue **mich** über das bestandene Zertifikat.
4. Die Polizei interessierte **sich** für den Vorfall.
5. Wir danken **euch** beiden für die Einladung zur Party.
6. Frau Glück und Herr Wein helfen **sich**.
7. Alexander putzt **sich** die Zähne.
8. Wir machten **uns** über den Jahresabschluss Gedanken.
9. Die Kontoauszüge lagen **durcheinander** auf dem Tisch.
10. Heute gehen wir **miteinander** ins Kino.

Exercise 8

1. Mit diesem Management wird das Unternehmen nie auf einen **grünen** Zweig kommen.
(With the present management this firm is getting nowhere.)

2. Alicée will immer die **erste** Geige spielen.
   (Alicée never wants to play second fiddle to anyone.)
3. Maria ist gerade noch einmal mit einem **blauen** Auge davongekommen.
   (Maria has managed to get off lightly again.)
4. Hier geht doch etwas nicht mit **rechten** Dingen zu.
   (Something definitely seems to be amiss here.)
5. Wir sollten das nicht an die **große** Glocke hängen.
   (We shouldn't make a big issue of it.)
6. Mike wurde mit **offenen** Armen empfangen.
   (Mike was welcomed with open arms.)
7. An dieser Aufführung hat der Theaterkritiker kein **gutes** Haar gelassen.
   (The theatre critic pulled this performance to pieces.)
8. Mit diesem Vorhaben hast du dir **kalte** Füße geholt.
   (You've got cold feet about this job.)
9. Das Ereignis traf uns wie ein Blitz aus **heiterem** Himmel!
   (The event hit us like a bolt from the blue.)
10. Dies sollte man nicht auf die **leichte** Schulter nehmen.
    (You shouldn't take something like this lightly.)

E x e r c i s e 9

1. groß:
   Eileen ist so **groß** wie Pia.
   Pia ist **größer** als Marcus.
   Tom ist von allen Praktikanten **am größten**.

2. gut:
   Herr Porter spricht so **gut** Deutsch wie Frau Hundt.
   Frau Hundt spricht **besser** Deutsch als Sarah.
   Gina spricht **am besten** Deutsch.

3. gesund:
   Limonade ohne Zucker ist **gesund**.
   Apfelschorle ist allerdings **gesünder**.
   Und ein Glas Wein am Abend ist **am gesündesten**.

4. viel:
   Über naturwissenschaftliche Erscheinungen wusste Inka **viel**.
   Über technische Neuerungen noch **mehr**.
   Und über sprachliche Angelegenheiten **am meisten**.

Exercise 10

1. Das habe ich mir **eben** vorgenommen.
2. Daran hat Vivian in der Eile **halt** nicht mehr gedacht.
3. Wo habe ich **bloß** meine Uhr hingelegt?
4. Was ist **denn** hier los!
5. Das ist **aber** großzügig von Ihnen!
6. Genau das habe ich **doch** gerade befürchtet!
7. Andy hat das **wohl** nicht so ernst genommen.
8. Dies konnte ich mir **ja** denken!

Exercise 11a

1. Am Montag hat Hardy eine Agenda für das nächste Meeting erhalten.
2. Von ihrem Mann hat Rebecca dieses Geschenk bekommen.
3. Um 10.30 Uhr nehmen die Touristen an einer Stadtführung teil.
4. Heute hat Yvonne einen Termin in der Autowerkstatt.
5. Den Gesprächstermin hätte Frau Simon wahrnehmen sollen.
6. Mit dem Bus fährt Margarita in die Stadt.

Exercise 11b

1. Gehe ich heute Abend mit Muriel in die Stadt?
2. Besuchen wir am Wochenende meine Cousine?
3. Muss ich mich am Samstag auf das Bewerbungsgespräch vorbereiten?
4. Treffen wir uns heute Nachmittag auf eine Tasse Kaffee?
5. Beschäfte ich mich gerade mit den Regeln der deutschen Grammatik?
6. Hat das Training bereits begonnen?

Exercise 12

1. **Kann** Andrew Deutsch sprechen? – Ja, er **möchte** aber seine Kenntnisse noch erweitern.
2. **Musst** du heute noch lernen? – Ja, ich **muss**!
3. Ich **darf** Ihnen doch bestimmt eine kleine Erfrischung anbieten, oder ...? – Ja, Sie **dürfen**.
4. Bitte beachten Sie, dass Sie auf Bahnhöfen nicht rauchen **dürfen**.
5. An dieser Stelle **dürfen** Sie nicht parken.
6. Du **möchtest** mit mir noch einige Worte sprechen?
7. Über das Jobsharing **müssen** wir uns nochmals Gedanken machen.
8. Hier **sollten** Sie leise sein.

Exercise 13

1. verfallen: Durch die Euro-Einführung **verfallen** bestimmte Briefmarken.
2. anfangen: Der Film „Harry Potter" **fängt** um 20.00 Uhr **an**.
3. übersetzen: Herr Brown **übersetzt** den Text ins Deutsche.
4. umschreiben: Der Trainer **umschreibt** die unbekannte Vokabel mit Synonymen.
5. abgeben: Der Kurier **gibt** das Paket an der Pforte **ab**.
6. umziehen: Am Sonntag **zieht** Pamela in die neue Wohnung **um**.
7. gefallen: Der Dom und die Steinerne Brücke in Regensburg **gefallen** mir.
8. ausfallen: Das Training-on-the-Job **fällt** heute **aus**.
9. unterstellen: Dieses böswillige Verhalten **unterstellte** man Kim.
10. zerfallen: Die Tagesordnung **zerfällt** in acht umfangreiche Punkte.

Exercise 14

1. Bewerben Sie sich **bitte** um den Job als Trainee!
2. Nimm **bitte** an dem Kurs in der Sprachenschule teil!
3. Rauchen Sie **bitte** nicht im Gang!
4. Frag **bitte**, wenn dir eine Redewendung nicht bekannt ist!
5. Kommt **bitte** pünktlich!

Exercise 15 a

1. Herr White buchte für Donnerstag einen Flug nach Deutschland.
   Herr White hat für Donnerstag einen Flug nach Deutschland gebucht.
2. Er kam am Flughafen Berlin-Tegel an und stieg in das nächste Taxi.
   Er ist am Flughafen Berlin-Tegel angekommen und [ist] in das nächste Taxi gestiegen.
3. Dieses fuhr Herrn White in das Hotel „Zum Goldenen Stern".
   Dieses hat Herrn White in das Hotel „Zum Goldenen Stern" gefahren.
4. An der Rezeption erhielt er die Schlüssel für sein Zimmer.
   An der Rezeption hat er die Schlüssel für sein Zimmer erhalten.
5. Um 15.00 Uhr traf sich Herr White mit seinen Geschäftspartnern.
   Um 15.00 Uhr hat sich Herr White mit seinen Geschäftspartnern getroffen.
6. Diese erklärten ihm die neue geschäftliche Situation und baten um Verständnis.
   Diese haben ihm die neue geschäftliche Situation erklärt und [haben] um Verständnis gebeten.

7. Herr White unterbrach die Verhandlungen und zog einen neuen Termin in Betracht.
Herr White hat die Verhandlungen unterbrochen und [hat] einen neuen Termin in Betracht gezogen.

8. Am nächsten Morgen holte Herr White seine Frau vom Flughafen ab.
Am nächsten Morgen hat Herr White seine Frau vom Flughafen abgeholt.

9. Gemeinsam verbrachten sie einige Tage in Berlin.
Gemeinsam haben sie einige Tage in Berlin verbracht.

10. Frau und Herr White sahen sich noch am selben Tag das Brandenburger Tor an.
Frau und Herr White haben sich noch am selben Tag das Brandenburger Tor angesehen.

11. Am folgenden Tag besichtigten sie den Reichstag.
Am folgenden Tag haben sie den Reichstag besichtigt.

12. Am letzten Tag ihres Urlaubs fuhren sie auf den Fernsehturm und warfen einen Blick auf die Dächer Berlins.
Am letzten Tag ihres Urlaubs sind sie auf den Fernsehturm gefahren und haben einen Blick auf die Dächer Berlins geworfen.

Exercise 15 b

1. **Nachdem wir einen Nachsendeauftrag bei der Post gestellt hatten,** fuhren wir in den Urlaub.

2. **Nachdem Eileen die Führerscheinprüfung bestanden hatte,** feierten wir das erfreuliche Ereignis mit einem Gläschen Sekt.

3. **Nachdem Marcus die Vor- und Nachteile dargestellt hatte,** gingen wir zur Aussprache über.

4. **Nachdem der Chef von seiner Auslandsreise zurückgekommen war,** wurde das umstrittene Projekt nochmals besprochen.

5. **Nachdem die Abteilungsleiter eingetroffen waren,** diskutierten wir über das weitere Vorgehen.

Exercise 16

1. Herr White wird für Donnerstag einen Flug nach Deutschland buchen.

2. Er wird am Flughafen Berlin-Tegel ankommen und [wird] in das nächste Taxi steigen.

3. Dieses wird Herrn White in das Hotel „Zum Goldenen Stern" fahren.

4. An der Rezeption wird er die Schlüssel für sein Zimmer erhalten.

5. Um 15.00 Uhr wird sich Herr White mit seinen Geschäftspartnern treffen.
6. Diese werden ihm die neue geschäftliche Situation erklären und [werden] um Verständnis bitten.
7. Herr White wird seine Verhandlungen unterbrechen und [wird] einen neuen Termin in Betracht ziehen.
8. Am nächsten Morgen wird Herr White seine Frau vom Flughafen abholen.
9. Gemeinsam werden sie einige Tage in Berlin verbringen.
10. Frau und Herr White werden sich noch am selben Tag das Brandenburger Tor ansehen.
11. Am folgenden Tag werden sie den Reichstag besichtigen.
12. Am letzten Tag ihres Urlaubs werden sie auf den Fernsehturm fahren und [werden] einen Blick auf die Dächer Berlins werfen.

Exercise 17a
1. Herr Miller sagt, er sei mit seiner neuen Marketingassistentin sehr zufrieden.
   (oder:) Herr Miller sagt, dass er mit seiner neuen Marketingassistentin sehr zufrieden sei.
2. Frau Dinz erläutert, durch das neue Computerprogramm könnten wir die Absatzzahlen schneller ermitteln.
   (oder:) Frau Dinz erläutert, dass wir durch das neue Computerprogramm die Absatzzahlen schneller ermitteln könnten.
3. Der Verkäufer erklärt, das neue Handy verfüge über eine USB-Schnittstelle.
   (oder:) Der Verkäufer erklärt, dass das neue Handy über eine USB-Schnittstelle verfüge.
4. Die Angestellte erwidert, durch mehr Personal erreichten wir eine bessere Kundenbindung (oder: … würden wir eine bessere Kundenbindung erreichen).
   (oder:) Die Angestellte erwidert, dass wir durch mehr Personal eine bessere Kundenbindung erreichten (oder: … erreichen würden).
5. Der Chef sagt, er sei mit der Arbeitsweise von Frau Gordon sehr zufrieden.
   (oder:) Der Chef sagt, dass er mit der Arbeitsweise von Frau Gordon sehr zufrieden sei.
6. Leyla fragt ihre Kollegin, für welchen Zeitraum sie ihren Urlaub eingeplant habe.

Exercise 17b

1. **Dürfte** ich Sie kurz stören?
2. **Könntest** du das für mich kopieren?
3. Das **wäre** wirklich nett von dir.
4. Ich habe keine eigene Firma. Aber wenn ich eine eigene Firma **hätte,** dann **würde** ich mit den Mitarbeitern jeden Morgen Tai-Chi **machen.**
5. So eine Katastrophe! Das alles **wäre** nicht **passiert,** wenn ich besser **aufgepasst hätte!**

Exercise 18

1. 2000 wurde Wladimir Putin zum russischen Staatspräsidenten gewählt.
2. 1999 wurde die NATO erweitert.
3. 1999 wurde Johannes Rau zum deutschen Bundespräsidenten gewählt.
4. 1998 wurde die Europäische Zentralbank eröffnet.
5. 1998 wurde die erste internationale Raumstation ISS aufgebaut.
6. 1993 wurde die Europäische Union eingerichtet.
7. 1991 wurde das Hubble-Teleskop gestartet.
8. 1990 wurden die beiden deutschen Staaten wiedervereinigt.

Exercise 19

1. Die Abschlussfeier fand bei **meinem Bruder Patrick** statt.
2. Der Autofahrer ist gegen **den Baum** gefahren.
3. Die Auszubildenden stehen im Kreis um **ihren Trainer**.
4. Aufgrund **der Globalisierung** werden Sprachkenntnisse immer wichtiger.
5. Die Touristen-Information befindet sich gegenüber **dem Rathaus**.
6. Trotz **der zahlreichen Regeln** beherrscht Axel die deutsche Grammatik gut.
7. Seit **einem Jahr** hat Steve einen Job als Webdesigner.
8. Während **der Sommermonate** befinden sich im Bistro um die Ecke nur wenige Gäste.
9. Ramona ist am Wochenende zu **ihrer Schwester** gefahren.
10. Der Bankangestellte holt das Geld aus **dem Tresor**.
11. Maggie und Geneviève haben für **den weltweiten Frieden** protestiert.
12. Der Schlüssel war zwischen **dem Gepäck**.

Exercise 20

1. Mike ist enttäuscht, **weil** die Vergütung nicht seinen Vorstellungen entspricht.
2. Peer wirkt gelassen, **seit** er täglich Joga-Übungen macht.
3. Lucia spielt seit drei Jahren Gitarre **und** [sie] surft auch gerne im Internet.
4. Victor freut sich, **dass** er nächste Woche in den Urlaub gehen kann.
5. Das Seminar fand nicht statt, **da** es zu wenig Teilnehmer gab.
6. Frau Wilice besichtigt das Deutsche Museum **oder** [sie] geht auf den Marienplatz.

Exercise 21

1. der Gummibaum
2. der Ringordner
3. das Druckerpapier
4. der Lichtschalter
5. der Schnellläufer
6. der Wohnungsmarkt
7. die Überbevölkerung
8. die Handytasche
9. der Nassschnee
10. das Hellblau
11. der Vorabend
12. das Zeitungsabonnement

Exercise 22

1. Simons Katze ist **entlaufen**.
2. Herr Franklin muss noch **einchecken**.
3. Marilyn ist krank und sollte sich daher **zudecken**.
4. Die **Reisefreiheit** war als wichtiger Fortschritt zu betrachten.
5. Das Bungeejumping sieht **gefährlich** aus.
6. Frau Setlur macht einen **jugendlichen** Eindruck.
7. Wir müssen das Geschenk **einpacken**.
8. Sollen wir Sie das Stück **mitnehmen**?
9. Auf dieses Angebot werden Sie bestimmt noch **zurückkommen**.
10. Die **Freundschaft** mit Jenny war mir viel wert.
11. Die **Assistentin** stellte das Projekt fertig.
12. Wir hoffen, dass Sie jetzt nicht mehr **sprachlos** sind!

Deutsches Register
German Index

Englisches Register
English Index